And Would You Believe It!

Some other books by Father Basset:

WE AGNOSTICS
WE NEUROTICS
NOONDAY DEVIL
HOW TO BE REALLY WITH IT
LET'S START PRAYING AGAIN
GUILTY O LORD

BERNARD BASSET, S.J.

And Would You Believe It!

Thoughts About the Creed

Doubleday & Company, Inc.   Garden City, New York
1976

Library of Congress Cataloging in Publication Data

Basset, Bernard.
    And would you believe it!

    Includes bibliographical references.
    1. Nicene Creed. I. Title.
BT999.B37   238'.142
ISBN 0-385-12164-4
Library of Congress Catalog Card Number: 76-3920

Dedicated to

A dear friend, John Delaney

who never guessed when he launched
the project that he would become
the inspiring image behind Image Books.

CONTENTS

The Nicene Creed

THE NICENE CREED

We believe in one God,
  the Father, the Almighty,
  maker of heaven and earth,
  of all that is, seen and unseen.

We believe in one Lord, Jesus Christ,
  the only Son of God,
  eternally begotten of the Father,
  God from God, Light from Light,
  true God from true God,
  begotten, not made, one in Being with the Father.
  Through him all things were made.
  For us men and for our salvation
    he came down from heaven:
  by the power of the Holy Spirit
    he was born of the Virgin Mary, and became man.

For our sake he was crucified under Pontius Pilate;
  he suffered, died, and was buried.
  On the third day he rose again
    in fulfillment of the Scriptures;
  he ascended into heaven
    and is seated at the right hand of the Father.
He will come again in glory to judge the living and the
  dead, and his kingdom will have no end.

We believe in the Holy Spirit, the Lord, the giver of life,
*   who proceeds from the Father and the Son.*
*   With the Father and the Son he is worshiped and glori-*
*   fied.*
*   He has spoken through the Prophets.*
*   We believe in one holy catholic and apostolic Church.*
*   We acknowledge one baptism for the forgiveness of sins.*
*   We look for the resurrection of the dead*
*   and the life of the world to come.   Amen.*

And Would You Believe It!

ONE

I Believe or *We Believe*

Left to my own devices, I might never have written this book. The creed has been dear to me since childhood, but I was beginning to feel that I had outgrown it, now that there is just one last article to be fulfilled. Should a policeman ask me what I am doing, I would say "Officer, I await the resurrection of the dead and the life of the world to come!"

When the first faint rumors about this book reached me, I felt an unusual weariness. It was the kind of fatigue experienced by the traveler after an extended journey by air. Who bothers with the spent counterfoils of a round-trip ticket, when one is comfortably seated for the last leg of the journey in a homegoing jet? For a moment, the articles of the creed seemed like those parts of the ticket that had done their job. I saw at once that such a simile was awry. Nowhere in Scripture is it suggested that God issues a series of tickets, each to cover a part of the journey and, then, to be thrown away. The image most common in Scripture is of a plant growing, be it a majestic cedar or a grain of wheat. We gardeners have to learn what the plants seem to know by instinct—that roots, stem, leaves, and blossom work together for the sake of the fruit. The Nicene Creed—or any other creed for that matter—follow this natural and supernatural plan. I could satisfy my policeman that I was awaiting "the life of the world to come" because my mother taught me to say "I believe in God, The Father, the Almighty" some sixty-five years ago.

This book came about because a good friend in New York, high in the publishing world and with many weighty volumes

14

in the market, chanced to ponder the Nicene Creed one Sunday at Mass. The brevity and clarity of the ancient creed arrested him. As he put it, "Time and again, I have thought in my own experience that in these few words is contained the real basis for Catholicism. Would you ever think of doing a book based on phrases from the creed and some discussion in your free and easy way? The more I have thought of it, the more enthusiastic I become about such a book."[1]

Though the creeds are the basis for the faith and their clarity helpful, they do not pretend to include all the theory and practice that make up Catholicism or Christianity today. To cover the whole story, one would need, at least, a modern catechism, incorporating modern changes, including the alterations added in Vatican Council II. Thumbing through various contemporary and bulky books, all very impressive, I slowly began to get my friend's point. Today, we need never to run short of information but we run the risk of being choked. What with synods, dialogues, charismatics, sharing—not to mention the dark shadow of such a topic as abortion—we may, in the general muddle, misplace God, The Father, Son, and Holy Spirit. The creed may not put last things last but it does put first things first. So I attempted the suggested book though feeling old and weary; the eternal verities do not alter much. I put aside the title that would have matched my mood exactly: *The Nicene Creed for Geriatrics. Granny, This Will Help You to Fall Asleep.*

Two other considerations stoked up my enthusiasm for this book. Each was associated with a greatly admired priest. The first, Monsignor Ronald Knox—Ronnie to all his friends in Oxford—retired to the country when his great days as university chaplain were done. He settled down to translate the entire Bible single-handed, an achievement that should have earned mention in *The Guinness Book of Records;* perhaps it has? Almost as remarkable as his translation of the Bible were the series of weekly lectures that he gave to a group of schoolgirls, moved from London to the country in World War II. Old, shy,

15

scholarly, Ronnie Knox dreaded this invasion but, when it had happened, he found his weekly sessions a rare delight. He was fascinated by the children, and they loved him. He gave a series of talks on the creed that he later published as *The Creed in Slow Motion* and, though he adapted his style to teen-agers, the book helped a great many adults as well. I found it stimulating at the age of forty and as fresh as ever when I was sixty-seven; I finished it last week. If there is no pleasure in following so gifted a scholar as Monsignor Knox, there is abiding consolation in sensing the timelessness and up-to-dateness of the old creed.

Monsignor Knox never fails to offer encouragement but it was another, even greater man, who made me change my mind. John Henry Cardinal Newman, slowly but surely, has made himself one of the greatest influences in life. Not only does Newman carry complete conviction in the field of personal religion, but I also find that he has the embarrassing gift of anticipating one's most personal and secret thoughts. Time and again, one discovers that so-called original thoughts, bright ideas, lights in prayer, personal inspirations that one never dared to mention, were set down by Newman with great precision more than a century ago. He is not the author of my book but, if I quote him often, this is because he is now almost the master of my mind. Newman—to use an ugly expression— was a creed man. Indeed, it would be difficult to name another writer as intensely committed to that form of prayer that our modern books prefer to name the profession of faith.

For Newman, any creed was a prayer or a hymn. He could not see the creed as a cold statement, a theological document, well above our heads. He writes of all the creeds, "they are devotional acts and of the nature of prayers, addressed to God and, in such addresses, to speak of intellectual difficulties would be out of place." Writing of the long Athanasian Creed, which was his favorite, he points out that it is not just a collection of notions but also a psalm. "It is a psalm or hymn of praise, of confession, self-prostrating homage, parallel to the

16

canticles of the elect in the Apocalypse. It appeals to the imagination quite as much as to the intellect. It is the war-song of faith . . . for myself, I have ever felt it as the most simple and sublime, the most devotional formulary to which Christianity has given birth, more so, even, than the *Veni Creator* or the *Te Deum*."[2]

In the later chapters of this book, we may consider various articles, but, here, in the Introduction, it is worth every effort to understand Newman's point. Any creed is a prayer. In much the same way as the "Marseillaise" was written as a song to sum up the French Revolutionary spirit without entering into constitutional details, so the creed expressed, for ordinary Christians, the spirit of the Church. It is not above our heads. As Newman pointed out, the word "mystery" is never used of any creed. Mysteries are there, but no creed was designed to examine these. The creed, as he says, was concerned with our personal reactions "and is not simply a statement of a mystery for the sake of its mysteriousness."

To understand the point more clearly, it may pay to examine briefly how the creeds came to exist. One ancient legend maintained that the Apostles penned the first formula, each of them composing one article. Though this is obviously far-fetched, there seem to have been various rudimentary creeds in existence from Apostolic times. St. Paul is thought to be referring to the creed when he writes to the Ephesians, "He made her clean by washing her with water with a form of words." (Ep. 5:26). These early creeds were certainly linked to baptism. The candidate for reception, normally adult, underwent a course of instructions and expressed his allegiance in some formula before the baptismal water was poured. In some cases, the candidate replied "Yes" or "No" to certain simple questions, much as we do in the Easter Vigil service today. The first creeds were a pact, an assent, a pledge of allegiance, and we should regard them thus today.

You may have noticed in the creed that we recite on Sundays how the Catholic Church, the forgiveness of sins, and

17

other final articles are crowded in and almost squashed together at the end. The explanation for this is easy, for they were added later; the original creed was addressed to Christ himself. One learned author suggests that the very first article, professing belief in God the Father, was an addition when the Council of Nicaea drew up the Nicene Creed. If so, this reaffirms that the earliest creeds were a personal pledge before baptism to the Son of God, made man. So small a detail may help to make the creed as a prayer more meaningful.

When Monsignor Knox lectured to the schoolgirls, he took the Apostles' Creed as his text. Here we deal with the Nicene Creed, for that was the version used for many centuries at Mass. Originally, both evolved from the same baptismal pacts. The Nicene Creed differs from the Apostles' Creed in this that it was sponsored by the Council of the Church that met at Nicaea in A.D. 325. The occasion was of high importance and the situation tense. The long persecutions of the Church were over, after occurring, savagely but sporadically, for close to three hundred years. Such a span of suffering should strengthen our patience today. The Council of Nicaea was the first General Council that we know of since the Apostles met in Jerusalem not long after Pentecost. The Roman Emperor Constantine had become a Christian, and the Church, for the first time, had freedom and could adjust to an open and public life.

The Fathers who came to Nicaea were almost all from what we might call the Middle East. Records are unreliable, but the great St. Athanasius, who was present, gives the number present as 318. Others make it less. There were groups of bishops from North Africa, Egypt, Palestine, and Asia Minor, with only a handful from the infant churches of the West. The Pope sent two representatives. Further details of the Council may be given later when we reach those articles that it added to the ancient creeds. It is sufficient here to note that, at the end of their debates, the Fathers recited together a profession of faith. It was rough and spontaneous, needed later adjustments, but has

18

enshrined the substance of the Christian belief for nearly seventeen hundred years. The fact that so many hundreds of saints, from East and West, across so many centuries have said it should enrich our recitation of the familiar words at Sunday Mass.[3]

One last small point should be considered before we turn to the content of the creed. The Apostles' Creed, I think, still starts with "I believe." For centuries, the Nicene Creed also opened with the singular but, in quite recent years, with the change to the vernacular, the translators switched to the first person plural, and we now say "We believe." Not a few faithful people were annoyed and puzzled and, in at least one Catholic periodical, a lengthy correspondence ensued.

If we view the controversy from a historical angle, the significance of the changes is slight. It so happens that the Fathers of Nicaea began their profession with "We believe in one God, the Father Almighty, creator of all things, visible and invisible." They made this alteration, it has been suggested, to express the unity of the Council, after a period of intense debate. Yet their change ran contrary to the ancient traditions of the baptismal creeds in which a candidate for Baptism personally committed himself. After the Council of Nicaea was over, the creeds reverted to the first person singular.

Historically, then, both sides in the controversy may claim to be right. If the Church of today asks us to use the first person plural, let us do so, without glancing swiftly to right and left at our immediate neighbors to decide whether or not we like their looks. If, for the sake of unity, the Council of Nicaea could switch from singular to plural, so may we. Psychologically—if this be the right word—the "I-We" question has puzzled me for years. Our Lord initiated the debate in words of one or two syllables when he quoted the Scriptures, "Thou shalt love the Lord, thy God with thy whole heart and thy whole soul and thy whole mind. This is the greatest of the commandments and the first. And the second, its like, is this, Thou shalt love thy neighbor as thyself." (Mt. 22:36). I find,

19

in Church history, two schools of thought, for there are those who worship God formally in Church but whose true love is for their neighbor, and through this love they reach God on a deeper grade. On the other side are the contemplatives, hermits, mystics, who love God first in solitude and, for his sake, are led to love their neighbor and to carry the love of God into their environment. Besides these two orthodox schools, one comes across a curious and dangerous imitation, possibly sponsored by Christian denominations, busy with groups and projects but not that much different from secular forms of philanthropy.

This third imitation needs to be watched in our present social climate with very great care. The choice between the two great commandments is our personal affair. But when we come to the recitation of the creed as a prayer, the motive behind it could be very different, between those who begin with "We" and those who say "I."

Monsignor Knox, in his lectures to those wartime schoolgirls, illustrates the choice. Notice that he was using the Apostles' Creed, which starts in the singular, and he was writing at a time when "We" had not been inserted into the Nicene Creed. I would like to quote you the full passage but have had to alter it slightly, for he used the Latin titles for the prayers at Mass. To the children he said "Let me direct your attention first to the use of the word 'I.' Surely that is curious if you come to think of it. Surely, saying the creed ought to be a tremendous congregational act, uniting us in a common profession of faith and, surely, at that rate it ought to start with 'We believe.' But it does not take that form. . . . If you watch the Gloria at Mass, it is 'we' all through—'we worship you; we give you thanks; we praise you for your glory.' We lose ourselves in the crowd when we are singing the Gloria. But when we sing the creed, we are not meant to lose ourselves in the crowd. Every clause of it is the expression of my opinion for which I am personally responsible. Just so with the 'I confess.' It is always 'I confess,' not 'We confess,' even when we are saying it together. Why? Because my sins are my sins and your sins are your sins; each of us is individually responsible. So it is with the creed; each of us in lonely isolation makes himself or herself responsible for that tremendous statement 'I believe in God.'[4]

"I expect you will think I have been making too much of that and rather wasting time over a minor point. Believe me, it isn't so. The reason why I want to give you this course of sermons on the creed is because I want each of you to say it intelligently, thinking of what you are saying, meaning what you are saying, not just copying the girl next to you, not just reciting a rigmarole of words that must be all right, of course, or the Church wouldn't make you say it. No, you are saying the creed as an expression of your own, individual point of view."

The Fathers gathered at Nicaea, although they expressed their faith in the plural for a special reason, would have agreed entirely with what Monsignor Knox has said. From the very beginnings of Christianity, the creed evolved as a personal response. As a witness in the courts takes his oath in the singular, as both bride and bridegroom in marriage commit themselves personally, so I alone can profess that I believe in God. The Nicene Creed provides the traditional framework, but we, in point of fact, make our own creed.

Let me end this Introduction with a private creed. Instead of calling it the Nicene Creed, we may name it the Birmingham Creed. "On January 17, 1865," as Cardinal Newman tells us, "it came into my head to write it. I really cannot tell you how. And I wrote on until it was finished on small bits of paper. And I could no more write anything else by willing it than I could fly." Newman was dead when Elgar composed the music for the Oratorio; he never heard "the Dream of Gerontius" and the creed at the start of it.

> Firmly I believe and truly
> God is Three, and God is One
> And I next acknowledge duly,
> Manhood taken by the Son.

TWO

We believe in one God,
the Father, the Almighty,
maker of heaven and earth,
of all that is, seen and unseen.

As the Nicene Creed sets out to express the basic beliefs of Christians, a detailed comment on every statement would require not one but at least twelve books. Hundreds of such commentaries exist in the sermons, letters, and learned writings of great theologians and saints.

In this small book, I hope to avoid too much detail in order to preserve the creed in its simplicity. More learned tomes report the discussions and debates to explain why this or that phrase was selected, but the creed, when it emerged, was intended for the ordinary man or woman in the street. As my friend from New York read the creed during Mass and was struck by its clarity, so the candidate for baptism in the early centuries recited it easily and willingly; in his day few had access to learned tomes.

As the creed was a prayer—psalm or war-song Newman called it—it should help us to raise up both mind and heart to God. Newman, you may remember, saw the creed as an act of devotion, attracting the imagination quite as much as the intellect. His point is important, and for this reason I would want first to guide your attention to the first two words, "I (or We) believe."

In the last chapter, I quoted Monsignor Knox speaking to those schoolgirls, and one sentence in it opened up an urgent question for me. He said to the children that the creed should not be recited as "a rigmarole of words that must be all right, of course, or the Church wouldn't make you say it"; such was certainly my attitude as a not too stupid boy. I now grasp the horrifying fact that such an attitude continued long after my schooldays were done. I do not think I was entirely free of it in the seminary or as a young priest. Further, I constantly meet the same attitude among good and mature adults. Once a charming young man, who was to marry a Catholic girl, presented himself and asked to be received into the Church. He said proudly, "I have had my instructions in my own parish" and produced a letter from his pastor to confirm the fact. Unthinking, I asked, "And did you believe the instructions?," at which he paused anxiously for a moment before replying "Yes, I think so; they seemed all right!"

Now, there is nothing whatever wrong in accepting the teaching of the Church and her authority; indeed, it may well be a great virtue, as I hope to show later in my book. On a lower level, we assume a similar attitude to our parents, to schoolmasters, to the government. There is, however, in everyday life a profound difference between acceptance and belief. I began to see this difference under the familiar labels of theory and practice until Cardinal Newman explained the problem in his *Grammar of Assent*.

It would be out of place in a book of this length to bog ourselves down with the intricacies of such a subject, but the conclusions now appear to me vital if we are to grasp what we mean when we say "I believe." Newman points out the difference not only between theory and practice but also between a notional and a real assent. A notional assent is made by the mind alone, and Newman describes the mechanism of the intellect, how it "makes a survey and catalogue of doctrines; it locates, adjusts, defines them each and brings them together as a whole." Elsewhere he points out that we speak of a process of reasoning, a chain of thought. The mind is like a computer, and when data are fed into it, it is able by deduction, classification, contrast, and generalization to hand us a conclusion on a plate. To such a conclusion, we may give a notional assent. But he adds in an aside, "Many a man will live and die upon a dogma; no man will be a martyr for a conclusion," and in this cryptic utterance we see the difference between acceptance and a real assent.

A real assent for Newman, as for all of us, is personal, not based on generalizations, useful and true as these may be. In the plane of religious experience, he points out the difference between the theological and the religious sense. Each assists the other, but they are not the same. Many great saints were not theologians, and many theologians were certainly not saints. Belief is a religious act, embracing the whole person, not just a notional assent. That is why he speaks of devotion when we recite the creed. "Devotion is excited by the plain categorical truths of revelation, such as the articles of the creed; on these it depends; with these it is satisfied. It accepts them one by one; it is careless about intellectual consistency; it draws from each of them the spiritual nourishment it was intended to supply."[1]

It just so happened that I was reading *Grammar of Assent* at the time the first American astronauts were heading for the moon. The comparison between these moon pioneers and the experts at Houston seemed at the moment to underline the difference between the real and the notional sense, for the men on the ground at Houston knew all about the moon, much about space, everything that could be known about the spacecraft; they could tell an astronaut when to sleep or wake and how to blow his nose. Their deductions were right, their skill immense, but they went home each evening to kiss their wives and to sip a martini with no real experience of the moon. The astronauts probably knew far less than their monitors at Houston, but they had seen and touched the moon.

As belief is the key word throughout the creed and "I believe" is supposed before each article, I would like to delay on its implications for a further space. The poor father in the gospel saw his son restored to health for his strange prayer was answered; he had cried out, in tears, "Lord, I do believe, succor my unbelief." (Mk. 9:24). Such sentiments should be ours when we say "I believe." Monsignor Knox put it this way to his children: "To believe a thing in any sense worth the name, means something much more than merely not denying it. It means focusing your mind on it, letting it haunt your imagination, caring desperately whether it is true or not." Belief, in other words, is a personal commitment, a real assent.[2]

It is more difficult for us today to master the true meaning because, in everyday conversation, people use the word carelessly. Sometimes they say "I believe" when they mean quite the opposite. Should someone say to me "Yes, I believe there is a train at ten-thirty," I know that he or she is not certain and that I had better check. At the grocer's recently, a housewife asked, "I believe you keep Danish bacon," but I could see by her expression that she was hazarding a guess. Or a mother says, "I believe he will pass his exam" when she really means "I hope he will." In much the same way we say at Mass "I believe in one God, the Father, the Almighty," while our heart entertains the question "Is this all make-believe?"

What belief meant to me in earlier decades, I cannot remember, for Cardinal Newman changed my whole outlook some twenty years ago. This remarkable man not only had learning, style, and precision, but also the experience of a long and lonely search for truth. Part of his influence is due to his unusual training, for he was, in turn, Evangelical, Calvinist, Church of England, founder of the High Church movement and, finally, Roman Catholic. Utterly sincere and earnest in each persuasion, he remained, in a sense, self-taught. Perhaps I should say God-taught, for there is, in Newman's approach, a depth of vision rarely to be found in other famous theologians or even in many saints. Newman was remarkably consistent; though, naturally, I rejoice that he became a Catholic, I do not praise him or follow him simply for that. His great sermons as an Anglican vicar are as helpful as any he preached in the Roman Catholic Church. Further, the seven or eight commanding ideas he retained and developed throughout a very long life. We say in the first article of the creed that we believe in God, maker of all things, seen and unseen and, to risk an Irishism, it was the unseen that Newman saw! Friends, disciples, and biographers touch on this insight, and the same will fascinate anyone who reads his letters, sermons, and books.[3] The artist Burne-Jones recalled, later in life, that he had learned from Newman "to venture all on the unseen."

With belief as our goal and the first article of the creed as guideline, let me give you the sentence from Newman that first halted me in my tracks. He wrote in *Grammar of Assent,* "I am as little able to think by any mind but my own as to breathe with another's lungs."[4] Such a statement sweeps away that passive acceptance by which we abandon all personal effort and simply believe whatever we are told. When I read Newman's words, I suddenly saw with shame that faith could be founded on secondhand sources in the manner of a lazy student's essay cribbed from imposing volumes and strung together with small personal effort or original thought. It is a sobering fact that even the teachings of Christ in the gospel will not avail me unless I apply myself and make them my own. The same would be true if my belief in the existence of God were based on the fact that St. Thomas Aquinas had worked out five proofs. As Newman put it, "The most authoritative of these three means of knowledge, as being specially our own, is our own mind."

If, like me, you sit back stunned, wondering what to do about it, Newman with no hesitation outlines a precise plan. "As in matters of this world, sense, sensation, instinct, intuition supply us with the facts and the intellect uses them, so in our relations with the Supreme Being, we get our facts from the witness, first of nature, then of revelation and our doctrines in which they issue, through the exercise of abstraction and inference."[5] No slight is intended when I point out that St. Thomas' five ways fall in the last category, with my senses, instincts, and intuitions coming first. Thus are we all designed and though, maybe, we were never told about it, St. Thomas and other great theologians said as much.

Stage One, in the Newman way, is to use your own mind and to have your own thoughts. Stage Two is to start your ascent with your own senses, sensations, instincts, and intuitions, a fascinating, do-it-yourself catechism course. It may take you some time to experience an effect, well known to artists, poets, saints, and mystics that we all possess interior and inward senses, parallel to the five physical ones, sight, sound, touch, taste, and smell. The inner senses may be part psychic, part spiritual. One significant point about them is that they are not intellectual deductions but experiences. Language itself seems to know about them; we speak of an ear for harmony, an eye for symmetry or beauty, a man or woman of good taste. Some people have a nose for scandal and not a few holy people were able to smell sin. Newman takes us one stage further than this. He insisted all through his life that our senses, sensations, instincts, and intuitions eventually lead us to an inner voice. I have only to write the word "voice" and every one of us thinks of conscience, which for Newman was "the connecting principle between the creature and his creator" and our firmest hold on truth.[6]

Let us turn now to the one God, the Father, the Almighty, maker of heaven and earth. The creed presents us with two aspects of his power, seen and unseen, and we make our ascent to him in two different ways. Through our five senses we amass more and more details about him throughout our lives. With the computer of our mind reaching conclusions, we come to know him, chiefly through his works. This approach is too involved for study here. The only point that I would stress is the extraordinary changes that have happened in my lifetime to this side of the Nicene Creed. Science has not only extended our universe and introduced the concept of evolution but also, through the advances in archaeology, biology, psychology, and Scripture studies, has shown us more about God than our ancestors ever knew. Do the words "the Father, the Almighty" mean for us what they meant when the bishops at Nicaea wrote them down? He was almighty then but, if it was not a

29

contradiction, I would say he is more Almighty now. Yet, in a century from now, we may be judged as fuddy-duddies and the Father, the Almighty, will be greater still. In fact, he does not change but, as mankind grows older and matures, it learns more about the subject, as do children moving up the school. Now, with the second approach, God does not alter at all. Nor do we, whose aspirations, sorrows, and hopes in the twentieth century are exactly expressed by the psalms that King David composed three thousand years ago. One might suggest that Almighty expands with each generation but that Father never changes, certainly not since the unique occasion when God sent his only son on earth. We may reach toward God by intellect and senses, but through the voice of conscience we experience God. Sometimes I say my own private creed, which begins "I believe in conscience," for such a profession brings one very close to God.

In his delightful little booklet *The Mind of Cardinal Newman,* Charles Stephen Dessain, the learned editor of Newman's letters, provides for the ordinary reader a neat collection of Newman's characteristic thoughts.[7] It pleased me to see that the cardinal's views on conscience were given pride of place. Any other arrangement would have been wrong, for there is no other subject that turns up so often in his sermons, novels, poetry, and books. I have to admit that it takes time and thought to grasp the full significance of Newman's arguments, but every effort is abundantly repaid. Believe that God speaks to you through your conscience and the creed itself ceases to be, in Ronald Knox's phrase, "a rigmarole of words."

Of all the passages about conscience, perhaps the most vivid is taken from a sermon that Newman preached twice. He first delivered it when he was Anglican vicar of St. Mary's, Oxford, and preached it again, with a few interesting alterations, when he was rector of the Catholic University of Dublin in 1856. I propose to quote a substantial passage, both for the content and for the precision of Newman's prose.

30

What is the main guide of the soul, given to the whole race of Adam, outside the true fold of Christ as well as within it, given from the first dawn of reason, given to it in spite of that grievous penalty of ignorance which is one of the chief miseries of our fallen state? It is the light of conscience, "the true Light," as the same evangelist says in the same passage, "which enlighteneth every man that cometh into this world." Whether a man be born in pagan darkness, or in some corruption of revealed religion—whether he has heard the Name of the Saviour of the world or not—whether he be the slave of some superstition—or is in possession of some portions of scripture and treats the inspired word as a sort of philosophical book which he interprets for himself and comes to certain conclusions about its teaching —in any case, he has within his breast a certain commanding dictate, not a mere sentiment, not a mere opinion, or impression, or view of things, but a law, an authoritative voice, bidding him do certain things and avoid others. I do not say that its particular injunctions are always clear or that they are always consistent with each other; but what I am insisting on here is this, that it *commands*—that it praises, it blames, it promises, it threatens, it implies a future and it witnesses to the unseen. It is more than a man's own self. The man himself has not power over it or only with extreme difficulty; he did not make it, he cannot destroy it. He may silence it in particular cases or directions, he may distort its enunciations, but he cannot, or it is quite the exception if he can, he cannot emancipate himself from it. He can disobey it, he may refuse to use it; but it remains.

This is conscience; and from the very nature of the case its very existence carries on our minds to a Being exterior to ourselves; for else whence did it come? and to a Being, superior to ourselves; else whence its troublesome peremptoriness? I say, without going on to the question *what* it says and whether its particular dictates are always as clear and consistent as they might be, its very existence throws us out of ourselves and beyond ourselves, to go and seek for him in the height and depth whose voice it is. As the sunshine implies that the sun is in the heavens though we may see it not, as knocking at our doors at night implies the presence of one outside in the dark who asks for admittance, so this Word within us, not only instructs

31

us up to a certain point, but necessarily raises our minds to the idea of a Teacher, an unseen Teacher; and in proportion as we listen to that Word and use it; not only do we learn more from it, not only do its dictates become clearer and its lessons broader and its principles more consistent, but its very tone is louder and more authoritative and constraining. And thus it is, that to those who use what they have, more is given; for beginning with obedience, they go on to the intimate perception and belief of one God.[8]

I trust you did not find this excerpt too long. For me it describes all the various stages, the inconsistencies, the commands that we cannot silence, the surrender to it that leads to the intimate perception of God. Each must be honest with himself. For me to deny conscience would be to deny the whole purpose of a lifetime; nothing is clearer than the basic admission by all human beings of right and wrong. Just a few psychopaths do not hear the voice of conscience, but these are abnormal; the verdict in a court of law admits this when it speaks of diminished responsibility. The data on which consciences are formed may vary greatly, and some of the details may be wrong. But the voice is there and the sense of responsibility and the groping toward a being other than oneself. You see this instinct even in very small children who, feeling ashamed, look for a wall on which they can bang their heads. There are those adults who explain conscience as a matter of upbringing, the monopoly of those who are religious-minded, which they themselves are not. Yet agnostics have skeletons in their cupboards and try to sweep the dirt under the mat. Conscience is active in everyone's life, even if many cannot admit it; such a refusal all too often ends with deep depression, heavy drinking, and trips to the psychiatrist's couch. Guilt is one of the most corroding agents in human life. Newman himself liked to refer to Lucretius, the great pagan philosopher who asserted "We should be happy were it not for that dreadful sense of religion which we all have, which poisons all our pleasures; I will get rid of it." Adds Newman, "But he could not and he destroyed himself!"[9] Jump two thousand years to get the other side of the story on the Gulag Archipelago. Solzhenitsyn wrote "Lying on the rotten straw in prison, I felt good stirring in me for the first time. I discovered that the dividing line between good and evil separates neither state nor class nor party but that it cuts through the heart of every man."[10]

Cardinal Newman had one short but important note to add. He corrects a mistake that I certainly entertained when I was younger and which, I suspect, is held by many others unwittingly. There is a danger of regarding conscience as a code of conduct in the same way as the Old Testament writers saw the Mosaic Law. Newman writes "Let us then consider conscience not as a rule of right conduct but as a sanction of right conduct," and this makes all the difference in the world.[11]

A simple and rather silly comparison helped me to see the cardinal's point. In the motoring world, it is the difference between the highway code and the warning lights on the dashboard of your car. The code is notional, collected by experts, supported by government authority, setting out a list of hazards and teaching us good motoring practices. The new driver has to know them, and all breaches may be penalized. Customs may vary from country to country, but, in general, the substance of motoring experience is much the same.

On the dashboard of each car—again one meets with variations—warning systems and safety gadgets have been introduced. Some are up-to-date and sophisticated, others old and primitive. These are not notional but real; they alert the driver and should not be ignored. I once sat for half an hour, during the rush hour, on an expressway outside Columbus, Ohio, while the driver, who had risked it, set out with a can to search for gas. On another occasion, with another friend, a little red light on the dashboard flickered until the driver stopped it with a bang. Lovely Annapolis was our goal that day, but we hardly saw it; we ate our picnic in a garage, gazing on the depressing back of another sucker's Chevrolet.

Newman saw the difference between the highway code and the gadgets on the dashboard; when he preached on conscience to the undergraduates in Dublin, he made the distinction in his last lines. Let me give you the whole sentence to round this chapter off: "Be sure, my Brethren that the best argument, better than all the books in the world, better than all that astronomy and geology and physiology and all the other sciences can supply—an argument intelligible to those who cannot read as well as to those who can—an argument which is 'within us'—an argument intellectually conclusive and practically persuasive, whether for proving the Being of God or for laying the ground for Christianity—is that which arises out of the careful attention to the teachings of our heart and the comparison between the claims of conscience and the announcements of the Gospel."[12]

THREE

We believe in one Lord, Jesus Christ,
the only Son of God,
eternally begotten of the Father,

We saw at the beginning of this book how the original creeds, including the Nicene Creed, which we say on Sundays, began as an act of allegiance before baptism. Such allegiance was pledged to one particular person, the "one Lord, Jesus Christ." Later, other beliefs were added, almost in a hurry, but two thirds of the Nicene Creed, as we now recite it, centers on the origin, office, birth, death, and resurrection of Our Lord Jesus Christ. If our creed is to be a prayer and not a catalogue of doctrines, we should preserve this personal approach.

Certain problems have occurred in the structure of this chapter, chiefly because the subject matter is so great. To understand the words of the creed, we need to think about Our Lord's incarnation, and this, in turn, requires an appreciation of revelation, which may be gained only by seeing what the world was like before revelations were made. Thus we go back and back until we arrive at conscience, which was for Cardinal Newman "the echo of God's voice." Rather than present you with many pages of unbroken print, I have decided to break this chapter into sections, each of which may stimulate thought and prayer. But these sections form one whole and may be seen as steps in the right direction, leading to that central article "We believe in one Lord, Jesus Christ."

First, before we start our ascent, we might pause for a moment to consider the Nicene Creed itself. Its structure and history have their interest, and a difficulty that worries certain people may be raised.

Cardinal Newman reminded us that the creeds were imaginative and simple, psalms rather than treatises. The suggestion may seem farfetched, but I am reminded of the creed when I watch TV each evening, for, almost nightly, from one country or another, we see shots of demonstrating crowds. All too often, alas, such crowds are politically organized and artificially angry, but even a hostile mob needs songs, slogans, and gestures to match its mood. Happily, we sometimes watch joyous crowds, welcoming home a hero, celebrating national independence, greeting a victorious team with a trophy held aloft. For Christians, the creed served in similar situations, and the allegiance that each member of the crowd had pronounced personally before baptism now became a collective rallying cry. In the olden days, many creeds were recited less often than they were sung. The Nicene Creed was, so it seems, added to the Mass for a special occasion in A.D. 589. A Visigoth King, Reccared, abandoned Arianism and proclaimed his conversion by reciting the Nicene Creed at Mass. It is of interest to note that he inserted it in the canon, just before the "Our Father," and in some Eastern rites the custom still pertains. The creed was regarded as a fitting preparation for those receiving communion at Mass.

Though the creeds were a simple form of prayer, stimulating and devotional, the discussions and debates before they were formulated were learned, acrimonious, and long. The arguments that led up to the Nicene Creed had been raging for a century. When the final decisions had been reached and tensions had lessened, the Fathers roughed out their creed. Maybe the bishops at Nicaea tossed their miters in the air and gave the V sign—for them the Sign of the Cross. At least they committed themselves irrevocably and publicly when they proclaimed together "We believe in one Lord, Jesus Christ."

Two questions puzzle some. Those who were cradle Christians wonder why it took so long to reach a decision on a subject that we accepted peacefully with our mother's milk. Even today, children and simple people find no problem in the divinity of Christ. We have to remember that, thanks to the

Council of Nicaea, the matter was settled and the doctrine defined. But the incarnation of God was unique, and they had no previous experience to guide them when questions were asked. As there will never be another incarnation, the problems will not occur again. For Christians, the only question since Nicaea and before it was the second coming of Christ. Early Christians—the Thessalonians, for example—expected Christ's return immediately. Throughout Church history scares and rumors have swept whole communities from time to time. As there will never be another incarnation, it fell to the Christians of the first centuries to decide what exactly is meant when we say that God became a man.

A second difficulty often occurs and was put to me recently by a friend who found it increasingly difficult to accept the Divinity of Christ. I cannot recall his words, but he maintained that as a boy and a young man, he never found any difficulty in accepting all the claims of Our Lord Jesus Christ. Christ was so obviously noble, his life simple, his teaching profound. In those earlier days, my friend was more worried about predestination, about eternal punishment, evil, the very existence of God. Now, in middle age, he has far less trouble in saying 'I believe in one God, the Father, the Almighty,' but more hesitancy in accepting that Jesus Christ was really and truly God. Let me make it clear that my friend retains his faith, that such a shift in problems is not uncommon, that his question is also asked by others, that I have experienced it myself. In my own case I am sure that Christian art, the cult of Christ's humanity in my boyhood tended to build up a Holman Hunt image of him, tender, nostalgic, but unreal. Eventually one must be of one's age, and then the long deliberations of the Fathers at Nicaea are explained. As much, even more faith is needed for the second article of the creed as for the first. Newman wrote "Next, I consider, in the case of educated minds, that investigation into argumentative proof of the things to which they have given their assent is an obligation or, rather, a necessity."[1]

38

THE ALTAR TO THE UNKNOWN GOD

In the story of the human race, one meets a constant desire
—call it expectation—that the denizens of heaven would make
contact and reveal themselves to man. Any study of mythol-
ogy, folklore, or comparative religion unveils this common
pattern in both East and West. For myself, who have been
able to pursue the subject only as a hobby, it came as a
surprise to discover in every civilization this same God-man
relationship. Recently, in a learned study of African tribal customs, one recognized patterns of thought found among the
Druids and Red Indians and also present in Greece and in ancient Rome. The variations were enormous, but the basic expectations were the same. Beyond the taboos, the magic, the
idols, evil spirits, and superstitions, there was a two-way
traffic, gods becoming men and men becoming gods. With due
solemnity, the Romans deified Caesar Augustus and a weird
bunch of assorted Emperors. At the very same time, Sts. Paul
and Barnabas had the shock of their lives at Lystra when the
crowd cried out "It is the gods who have come down to us in
human form." When the local priest arrived complete with
bulls for sacrifice, I would have loved to have seen the expression on Paul's face.

In the pagan world, a shallow concept of incarnation was a
commonplace. If much religious thought was childish, even
evil, one comes across exceptionally noble and, possibly, holy
people with profound, penetrating thought. How surprised I
was when, at seventeen, I was studying Virgil to find that the
pagan poet had come near to the language of the gospel of St.
John. Marcus Aurelius, the Emperor and stoic, had moved far
beyond the state religion; his Fate or Providence came pretty
near to God. Or you read in the Bhagavad—Gita "Certainly
man is the master of his own destiny. He has free will—the
greatest of God's gifts to him, whereby he has complete free-

39

dom of action. But having performed an action, he has to bear its consequence."

I make no excuse for delaying so long on what may seem to you a remote subject; could I say "I believe in one Lord, Jesus Christ" without noticing the difference between his incarnation and the natural religion of fallen man. Newman writes "Wherever religion exists in a popular shape, it has invariably worn its dark side outwards,"[2] for the pagan religions were all full of fear. Fear of punishment after death was well nigh universal—Virgil outstripped Dante in his pictures of Hell. Sacrifices, animal and human, were used continuously to make atonement to gods who were often evil, by men who had no clear views about sin. We may smile at the ancient antics but among modern pagans I have seen some strange experiments in my day. From flying saucers to astrology and the cult of spiritism, devil worship, and now pyramids. I have lost count of the messiahs, one of them fifteen and with a peptic ulcer, who came to us if not from heaven, at least from California.

The spirit of the pagan world is best captured in ancient Athens, one of the most sophisticated cities in the world. When St. Paul visited Athens, as St. Luke tells us, the Apostle first toured the city and came home exasperated at its widespread idolatry. Yet, when he faced the prestigious audience in the Court of Areopagus, Paul opened gently with much understanding and sympathy. His masterly address began "Men of Athens, wherever I look, I find you scrupulously religious. Why, in examining your monuments as I passed by them, I found among others an altar that bore the inscription to 'The Unknown God.' And it is this unknown object of your devotion that I am revealing to you." (Ac. 17:22).

St. Paul's address was not received too well. Some laughed, a few said "See you later"; only a handful, Dennis and a woman called Damaris among them, "attached themselves to him." Paul's punch words, "judgment repentance, resurrection through this man Jesus," fell on deaf ears. Yet the scene in

Athens comes to life when we grasp that the unknown God of the Athenians was the same God we know by conscience and that Paul was preaching one of the very first sermons on the creed.

CONSCIENCE AND THE GOSPEL

In the last lines of the previous chapter, I quoted Newman's message to the Dublin students that "the comparison between the claims of conscience and the announcements of the gospel" provides the strongest of arguments. Take conscience first, a voice that I discover entirely through my senses, sensations, instincts, and intuitions; a voice personal to me. Each one for himself in the interpretation of his conscience; no one else in the world is able to translate its message or to break its code. A friend told me that he said his prayers because of conscience; another might declare himself a conscientious objector; when many of his clerical friends were marrying, John Henry Newman—I think because of conscience—remained celibate. Conscience is personal; my money is on Hamlet and his vital verdict, "Thus conscience doth make cowards of us all."

The creed acquires a meaning for those only who admit life's basic fears. I have lived too long, read too much history, met too many frightened people, to water down the fears of existence in the hearts of us all. Yes, there are physical fears, mental fears, moral fears, casting long shadows before them; nagging for many years before we ask the timid question, "Doctor, is it terminal?"

Nor is conscience reassuring; a voice always in the present moment, as immediate in its message as the voice of a caller on the phone. Newman admits that there are those who try to stifle conscience, who attempt to run their moral life purely by intellect. These ignore the senses, sensations, instincts, intuitions, and the voice that these reveal. For them moral evil derives from the physical, knowledge is virtue, prayer superstition, fear of God unmanly, sorrow slavish; "that if we do

our duties in this life, we may take our chances in the next."
Very good luck to them!

If I quote Newman often and rely on him, always, this is explained by the satisfaction he gives me in maintaining truth boldly even when it appears unfashionable. It is unfashionable to preach the fear of God today, to admit that we must answer for our actions, yet Newman does not hesitate to inform us that conscience tells us so. His words are blunt: "Conscience suggests to us many things about that Master, whom, by means of it, we perceive, but its most prominent teaching and its cardinal and distinguishing truth is that he is our judge. In consequence, the special attribute under which it brings him before us, to which it subordinates all other attributes, is that of Justice—retributive justice. . . . And when the time comes, which conscience forebodes of our being called to justice, we shall have to stand in and by our-selves, whatever we shall by that time have become and must bear our own burdens."[3]

The pagans knew this. Though many of their gods were disreputable, they offered to them sacrifices of atonement because, as men, they had a conscience and knew fear. The altar to the unknown God at Athens was an anxious gesture by sophisticated people who did not feel too sure.

One short passage from Genesis puts the lesson of conscience into the proverbial nutshell whether we are religious or not. In the evening, God walked in the garden of Eden while Adam and Eve hid in the bushes until he called them out. When Adam blurted out "I was afraid because of my nakedness so I hid myself," God posed the fateful question, "Who told thee of thy nakedness?"

I doubt very much whether anyone saying the creed could really mean it, if he or she had confidence in himself or herself. Far be it from me to condemn pride in our work, satisfaction in our talents and achievements, to suggest that we must perpetually hang our heads, dress in black, and talk like Uriah Heep. Yet we must admit in our hearts, through the light of conscience, that no matter how high the opinion of us

42

by others, we can do little or nothing by ourselves. To say "I believe in one Lord, Jesus Christ" implies "I *dare* not believe in myself."

This unconditional surrender freely executed, the picture appears not so black. Both St. John the Baptist and St. Paul began their revelations with judgment and repentance but ended on a happier note. St. Paul at Athens spoke of resurrection; John, in the deserts of Judaea, promised good news. Conscience itself tells us more of God than his retributive justice; our fear of him in conscience is home-made and derives from self-analysis. Behind the fear of existence is a sense of hope and purpose, an aspiration that Newman describes as a thirst. I would like to quote you Newman's own words, for they are helpful, especially where the comparison between conscience and the lessons of the gospel are concerned. Preaching on conscience, he remarks, "In spite of all that this voice does for them, it does not do enough, as they most keenly and sorrowfully feel. They find it most difficult to separate what it really says, taken by itself, from what their own passion and pride, self-love and self-will mingles with it. Many is the time when they cannot tell how much that true inward Guide commands and how much comes from a mere earthly source, so that the gift of conscience raises a desire for what it does not itself fully supply. It inspires in them the idea of authoritative guidance, of a divine law and the desire of possessing it in its fulness, not in mere fragmentary portions or indirect suggestions. It creates in them a thirst, an impatience for the knowledge of that unseen Lord and Governor and Judge, who as yet only speaks to them secretly, who whispers in their hearts, who tells them something but not nearly so much as they wish or as they need."[4]

Revelation means so much more when it is linked to conscience; the Bible faces us with problems, which, somehow, we feel that we have met before. Let me explain the point through a juvenile example for you, maybe, have also suffered keen frustration in trying to solve a problem, be it a crossword puzzle or one of those checkmate-in-three moves that they set in chess. You stare for hours in vain. Of a sudden, frustration changes to fascination when an expert sits beside you and resolves the problem in a trice. When I sit at my spiritual chess board, I find it helps greatly if Moses or King David is at hand. Such massive mysteries as guilt, sin, atonement, evil, even predestination, which tax the conscience, are halfway to solution if we read the Bible sensibly.

Faith is an incomparable gift that carries one disadvantage for those who received it early and too easily. There is a temptation to sit back complacently, to pity the plight of the poor, misguided pagans, ignorant of the answers that the Church has known for two thousand years. Maybe a similar conceit damaged many of the ancient Israelites. In one sense, we are in the greater danger, for the Bible today is neatly arranged and bound in vellum; with the smugness of a museum curator we are able to exhibit the whole of revelation, between two covers, to an inquirer. Conscience saves us, for the thirst and desire we have to know our master makes the Bible a personal treasure and ourselves the inquirer.

Maybe you were more lucky and saw the link between conscience and revelation at an early age. Though I won many prizes for Scripture exams, I never saw any connection between the Old Testament and my personal religion when I was at school. The masters were learned enough and I was clever enough, but I had not yet heard of Newman or memorized Hamlet's statement that conscience makes cowards of us all. I have since discovered that Cardinal Newman wrote on this very point. At the time when Bible reading was in vogue and the very peak of religious practice, he was bold enough to declare, as a great lover of the Bible, that such reading "is not a religion of persons and things, of acts of faith and of direct devotion but of sacred scenes and pious sentiments . . . it induces its followers to be content with a meagre view of revealed truth."[5]

Link conscience to the Bible, and the Old Testament comes

alive. The God who speaks to me secretly in my heart, speaks to Cain as he tells a lie, to young Samuel in the Temple, to David, fasting and prostrate on the floor, pleading for his infant son. As the incarnation of Christ draws near, the tempo of the story changes, and strange hints and hopes about "my servant" coming, start to appear. Faint reflections of God's private life appear in the Book of Wisdom, if I may describe so great a mystery in that way. We should note the difference between Scripture study and Scripture meditation; the second involves sense, sensation, instinct, intuition, conscience, all that is personal to each one.

Yes, I studied Scripture at one time, drew maps of Palestine, memorized the measurements of Solomon's Temple, even learned a little Hebrew, to no purpose, I regret, in this world or the next. Now I read no footnotes, but I treasure the Old Testament. In my private creed, I say "I believe in conscience! I believe in revelation"; both essential if you are ever to say with meaning "I believe in Jesus Christ our Lord."

Every now and then, pacing my room, I smile. I smile as a roaring Roman Catholic, who now has two statues of Moses in his very small rooms. In the living room, a replica of Michelangelo's famous sculpture forms the stem of a desk lamp; in Exodus, after meeting with God on Sinai, Moses' radiance came from heaven; now, alas, he must make do with a hundred-watt bulb. But in my private room, where most of us keep our conscience, young Moses lies prostrate before the burning bush.

LORD, I BELIEVE; HELP MY UNBELIEF!

I have quoted this text before, the prayer of an unnamed but distracted father, who had brought his son to Jesus, the boy convulsed and frothing at the mouth. When Christ said "All things are possible to him who believes," the distressed father came out with the words just quoted, "Lord, I believe; help my unbelief." Monsignor Knox prefers "succor my be-

45

lief," a phrase slightly outdated, but adding a nuance that I like but cannot explain. The prayer in itself is both humble and expressive, making allowance for what we might call a double-think. How hard it would be to state the thought behind it in a simple sentence, and yet, we know from our own experience exactly what he means.

This poor father's prayer may aptly introduce this next, short section, leading up to our profession "We believe in one Lord, Jesus Christ." It deals with the meaning of *belief* as this affects us personally when we face the mystery of the incarnation of the Son of God, made man. Were the incarnation to be proved untrue, Christianity would be ended, though millions would continue to love and admire Jesus Christ. I do not know why they would for, if his claims were false, he would have shown himself the very imposter that they accused him of being on the Cross. Somehow we cannot think of Christ as an imposter; some dictionaries cleverly skirt around the issue; they define a Christian as one who follows the example and precepts of Jesus, failing to mention that he claimed to be the Son of God.

One curious problem meets us in the gospels, that some people accepted Christ at once and others did not. Both groups saw the same man, heard the same words, witnessed the same signs and wonders, met the same kindness, received the same promises but reacted differently. The Jewish attitude to Jesus illustrates the point. Unlike the pagans, with their multitude of gods, the Israelites had been remarkably faithful, maintaining the Law as given to Moses and the covenant made by God with Abraham. True, there were backslidings on occasions—the prophets did not mince matters—but, all said and done, the Jewish record of fidelity is unique in ancient history. What is more, the Hebrew Scriptures had long foretold the coming of a Messiah, the anointed one. Admittedly, there existed some confusion about his office, for national and political aspirations fused with the spiritual. Expectations ran high. Yet when Jesus appeared among them, some immediately accepted him as the promised Messiah; others rejected him outright and eventually organized his shameful death. It would be easy enough to explain this rejection by blaming the ruling clique. Envy, prejudice, greed, as always, had their parts to play. We find the same self-interest throughout Church history down to our own day. Just as many of his own people rejected Jesus, so do many one-time Christians in this age. I am not thinking so much of nominal Christians, babies who are christened in church and never enter it again. Recently, I performed a baptism with the new rite, rich in promises and symbols; the service was halfway through before I realized that the baby and myself were the only practicing Christians in the place! In our urban conglomerations, there are bound to be many, of all denominations, who are nominal Christians and no more. Yet, just as the Jews rejected Christ and his claims, so do Christians from devout homes, educated in the faith, who sang the creed with feeling for many years. Now, in middle age, they have lost interest in Christ and his claims. Of their once ardent faith, only a certain secret nostalgia remains. Why does Christ succeed so swiftly in some cases and in others slowly fail? Why, in ancient Athens, did Dennis the Areopagite and Damaris say "Yes" to Paul when the rest of the audience said "No"? Or, for that matter, why did Ernest Renan shed his soutane and St. Sulpice three days before John Henry Newman, with so much anguish, was received into the Church at Littlemore? Individual cases need special study and a personal answer, but I would like to propose one general observation that helped me greatly in reading the gospel and added much to the recitation of the creed.

Faith, as we know, is always a gift from God. The old catechism still supplies the shortest and best definition: "Faith is a supernatural gift of God that enables us to believe without doubting whatever God has revealed." God had the free disposal of this gift which, because it is above nature, is out of the reach of the natural man. Man is only able to grope toward it, and many did. The Emperor Marcus Aurelius came very near,

47

and his *Meditations* were much used by many Christians; the Roman poet Virgil was regarded in ancient times as a pagan, John the Baptist and was allotted a feast day in some Christian communities. Faith was a gift, and God seemed to give it as he pleased. He gave it surprisingly to that fanatical Pharisee, Saul, on the road to Damascus and, understandably, to a retired clergyman living in isolation outside Oxford, at Littlemore.

I wrote just now that God gives the gift of faith as he wills. Such a statement is true and yet Newman, as always, probes deeper, to sketch out the active part that we human beings have to play. He explained from the pulpit once "In describing that state of mind and thought which leads to faith, I shall not of course be forgetting that faith, as I have already said, is a supernatural work and the fruit of divine grace. I shall only be calling your attention to what must be your part in the process."[6] He went on to outline the dispositions needed before God will grant the gift of faith. The plain fact is that God, though almighty, is always courteous, fully respects the freedom of the individual, and grants the gift of faith to those who so wish.

As always with Newman, we are back to the voice of conscience and to the God whose voice it is. This time, however, we concern ourselves with human beings and the two attitudes to conscience that people take. First, there are those who recognize the truth of conscience and, with some fear, accept their responsibility. They admit to their nakedness, unconditionally surrender, and experience the first faint stirrings of hope. Grasping with astonishment that the God of their conscience loves them, they develop this great thirst. Thirst for the truth is the first disposition needed for the gift of faith. The second follows from this, for they are always on the *lookout;* when he printed his sermons, Newman used italics, perhaps to impress the lesson, perhaps because the word was new in his world. Both words, "thirst" and "lookout," deriving from conscience, exactly express our contribution to the gift of faith.

The contrary attitude to conscience is obvious. Few are able to suppress its voice or to avoid occasional twinges, but neglect or inattention are possible. Those who neglect their conscience are never on the lookout, because they are well contented with themselves. Such may be pagan, Jew, or Christian, but what religion they have is notional. They may believe in God as a boy accepts Euclid; true, but of no immediate concern. For them, there is much theory but no commitment, no searching after truth. Describing the two attitudes, Newman summed up this way: "The one goes to meet the truth; the other thinks that the truth ought to come to him. The one examines into the proof that God has spoken; the other waits until this is proved to him."[7]

When we read the gospels, we meet countless examples of these two attitudes. Further, we find that Christ rarely if ever distinguished between faith and no faith but between great faith and little faith, between hardness and easiness. When he cried out, after the parable of the sower, "Those who have ears to hear, let them hear," he had these two attitudes in mind. In phrase after phrase, when he praised the faith of those who came to him, he seemed to see this easiness of acceptance as a distinguishing mark. He said to one "O woman, great is thy faith," and to another, "Be of good heart, daughter, thy faith has made thee whole." The centurion, who was a pagan, bowled Christ over with his faith; the centurion did not even ask for the personal satisfaction of a visit; enough for him that Jesus should say the word. Christ, who was a Jew and who knew the long-enduring faith of his own people, yet put this pagan first. He said with his fellow countrymen around him, "I have not found faith so great in Israel."

St. John the Baptist is far more important in the gospel story than many recognize. When the invisible God sent his son on earth, he needed someone to go before him to prepare the way. Why? Because the two dispositions for faith—the thirst for truth and a heart ever on the lookout—must be present for a living faith to thrive. John—greater, as Christ said,

49

than any of the previous prophets—performed his function gloriously. If you examine his sermons in the desert, you feel he must have read Cardinal Newman, for he linked conscience, sorrow, and repentance to the gospel scene. For all his thunder, he promised good news and promised hope, but he pointed out the unknown man in the crowd who alone could satisfy the need. At the very start, Jesus did not call Peter, Andrew, James, and John; they first called on Jesus. How immediate and easy was their faith. Christ himself was surprised at Nathaniel's acceptance, "What, believe because I told you that I saw you under the fig tree? You shall see greater things than that."

If examples of easy acceptance of Christ are plentiful in the Gospel, such acceptance was made by men and women of the same type. Some were Jews, some pagan, some honorable, and some sinful, but all were thirsty for the truth. How different were the people on the other side. Hardness of heart was the charge that Christ leveled against them and, of course, hypocrisy. Where Peter, Zacheus, Magdalen, and others were overwhelmingly grateful to Jesus, Simon the Pharisee and Judas Iscariot were not. Indeed, those who finally rejected Christ thought that by listening to him or inviting him to dinner, they were doing favors for him. Most knew the Scriptures well and respected the laws of Moses, but they utterly lacked the two dispositions for faith. In Jesus' own village of Nazareth he was not accepted, "nor did he do many miracles there because of their unbelief." They wanted to make a bargain with him and he objected: "Unless you see signs and wonders, you do not believe." Never for a moment did they think of the Messiah but saw Christ as a politician bargaining for votes. When you think of it, the different attitudes to conscience after the Incarnation changed to two different attitudes to Christ.

I wonder why Christ chose one of the apostles to bring home to us this point. One feels sorry for St. Thomas, for he was faced with the resurrection, surely the supreme test ever known to man. But when he set his conditions for belief and used words like "unless" and "until" to limit his acceptance, he taught us a lesson that we should never forget. Christ's answer to Thomas reveals to us many secrets "You believe because you can see me; happy are those who have not seen and yet believe."

BACK TO NICAEA

We believe in one Lord, Jesus Christ,
The only Son of God,
Eternally begotten of the Father,
God from God, Light from Light,
True God from true God,
Begotten, not made,
Of one Being with the Father
Through him all things were made.

In the final section of this chapter, I suggest that we return to the actual words of the creed that we recite on Sundays, words added by the Fathers of Nicaea to meet an emergency. Many other articles of the creed deal with the Incarnation, so we may return to the gospel, to the life and death of Jesus in the chapters ahead. The Council of Nicaea inserted all these clauses before the Incarnation had been mentioned that all might accept Christ's divine status from the start.

Two facts are certain from New Testament evidence, the first that Jesus Christ was truly a man. The people of his neighborhood knew his family and relations; the villagers from Nazareth said "Is not this the carpenter's son, whose mother is called Mary?," and they can speak for all the rest. Those who rejected him were doubly certain of his manhood when they watched him die. After the Resurrection, a second certain fact emerges, that those who saw him knew that he had proved his assertion that he was the Son of God. Four of the eleven apostles who had been with him since those first days in Galilee

51

now wrote letters to various Christian communities, and one may sense the changes wrought in them by their very words. Jude, warning his friends against troublemakers, begs them "to make your most holy faith the foundation of your lives." Today, we tend to accept the myth that the early Christians were all saintly, chanting "Alleluia" and speaking interminably in "tongues." St. Paul's two letters to the Corinthians open our eyes to the facts. There were many scandals and many mischiefmakers, but the primitive Christians, with heroic effort, lived and died for a common faith. What was this faith?

I am almost able to see the wan smiles on many faces when John Henry Newman reappears. You might be tempted to ask what a Victorian Oxford parson is doing in the first four Christian centuries, and the answer must be that he was searching for the truth. As a young Oxford tutor, distressed with the lax religious opinions of the day, the liberalism of the established Church, the superstitions of Rome as he, then, saw them, Newman went back to the primitive centuries, studied them in detail, and wrote fascinating accounts of Anthanasius, Basil, Gregory, and the great Christian leaders, sketches well worth attention today.[8] He wrote of conscience in this time of mental distress, "Were it not for this voice, speaking so clearly in my conscience and my heart, I should be an atheist, or a pantheist or a polytheist when I look into the world."[9] There can be no doubt that these earnest years of study had a profound effect on Newman's religious thought. In a book of this size, a few of his conclusions will prove more useful than any attempt to synopsize five hundred years of complex history.

1. From the very start of the Church, belief was founded on the doctrine of the Holy Trinity. "First of all," says Newman, "the teaching of the Fathers was necessarily directed by the form of baptism, as given by Our Lord himself to his disciples after the resurrection. To become one of his disciples was, according to his own words, to be baptised "in the name of the Father, and of the Son, and of the Holy Ghost." Such was Our Lord's injunctions; and ever since, before Arianism and after,

52

down to this day, the initial lesson in religion, taught to every Christian, on his being made a Christian, is that he belongs to a certain *Three,* whatever more, or whether anything more is revealed to us in Christianity about that *Three.*" Many witnesses prove this point, the most glorious, St. Polycarp, St. John's disciple, who ended his last prayer before execution "I glorify Thee, through the Eternal High Priest, Jesus Christ, Thy beloved Son, through whom be glory to Thee, with Him and in the Holy Ghost, both now and forever."

2. During the centuries of persecution, despite much suffering, this central Christian doctrine was sturdily maintained. Erroneous views held by some—St. John mentions the first in his second letter (2 Jn. 1:7)—did not spread widely in the underground Church. One or two of the phrases, now part of the Nicene Creed, "begotten of the Father," may have derived from this earlier period. With the conversion of the Emperor and the emancipation of the Church, controversy became public, the state interfered, and bishops were recognized as important political figures, for which reasons Arianism spread rapidly through the Eastern world. Yet Newman asserts that Arianism was not a popular heresy: "The laity, as a whole revolted from it in every part of Christendom. It was an epidemic of the schools and of theologians and to them it was mainly confined. It did not spread among the parish priests and their flocks or the great body of the monks. . . . The classes which had furnished martyrs in the persecutions, were in no sense the seat of the heresy."

Newman himself was a highly intelligent man, but, as we have seen already, he retained throughout his life a fear of generalizations and deductions, especially where personal religion was concerned. Notional assents could be a help to religion but not religion itself. I often wonder if the Arian disputes between the theologians of Antioch and Alexandria fashioned his future views.

3. The names of all the disputants are highly confusing, and one feels as lost as a traveler in a foreign bus station searching

for the right bus. There were Arians, semi-Arians, Nestorians, Apollinarists, Eutychians, Monophysites, Docetists, Sabellians, and heaven knows how many more. We could afford to smile at them were it not for an equally long list of sects at the time of the Protestant reformation or in any large Western city today. The heretics of the fourth century were all concerned with the incarnation and the Christian belief that the Son of God became a man. The extremists on one wing maintained that Jesus, the man, was purely an apparition; far out on the other wing were the Arians, who asserted that Christ was a man, selected as a Messiah by God. In between were those who admitted that Christ was God but that he had been created, for which reason the Nicene Fathers added "begotten, not made." The key phrase "of one being with the Father" made explicit that the three Persons of the Holy Trinity were truly and substantially God.

4. The Nicene Creed, through all those curious and yet similar phrases strung together, asserted what Christians had believed from the first. Nicaea had the first but not the last word. St. Cyril would later re-emphasize the point. The final and clearest statement, which greatly pleased Newman, was made by Pope St. Leo the Great, whose letter to Flavian on the subject was read at the Council of Chalcedon in A.D. 451. I quote a passage, as this best sums up what the Nicene Creed intends to say. Leo confirms that there are two natures in Jesus Christ—the Monophysites postulated only one, "For each nature without defect preserves its proper characteristics and, as the form of a servant does not take away the form of God, so the form of God does not diminish the form of a servant. . . . Each form, in union with the other, does what is proper to it: The Word, that is to say, operating that which is proper to the Word and the flesh performing that which is proper to the flesh. . . . The divine nature shines forth in miracles, the human nature succumbs to injuries. And as the Word does not fall away from equality with the Father's glory, so the flesh

54

does not leave the nature of our race. For one and the same, a point often to be repeated, is truly God and truly son of man . . . to hunger, to thirst, to be weary and to sleep is, evidently, proper to man. But to satisfy five thousand men with five loaves and to give the woman of Samaria living water is, without doubt, divine. It does not belong to the same nature to say "I and the Father are one" and again "the Father is greater than I."[10]

When the Fathers at the Council had heard the statement, they cried out "That is the Faith of the Fathers; that is the faith of the Apostles. So we all believe. Peter has spoken through Leo."

So the great controversy was decided. Our Lord was consubstantial with the Father; one Person with two complete natures, one human, one divine. I had to abbreviate St. Leo's letter slightly, but I hope that you will find it helpful in the next chapter, when we consider Christ dying on the Cross. St. Leo's letter also helps us to understand the nature of a creed. After all the years of argument, after so many inferences and deductions clearly stated, nothing was added that Peter, James, John, and Jude, with their companions, had not believed nearly four hundred years before.

5. In his most famous book, *The Apologia,* John Henry Newman set out the story of those spiritual struggles, which took him back to study the faith of the early Christian Church. He knew so much about the great Eastern saints Athanasius and Basil, wrote about "the majestic Leo," and suddenly grasped that he, Newman, was on the wrong side. Of the view that he had been following he wrote "Down had come the Via Media as a definite theory or scheme, under the blows of St. Leo."[11] Two pages earlier came the celebrated and startling statement "I saw my face in that mirror and found that I was a monophysite."[12] After all the work, all the thought, all the study, he had missed the full meaning of the incarnation, had allowed Christ not two but one nature, and had never grasped

55

what it meant to say that the only son of God had become a man.

Newman wrote much about conscience because, through a long life, he heeded the voice of conscience as the echo of God's voice. He knew little of Catholicism, and that little did not attract him; six years later he was received into the Church at Littlemore. If he took so long to grasp the reality that Christ was truly a man, maybe we too need to think deeply before we recite the Nicene Creed.

EPILOGUE

I wind this chapter up on a completely different subject but one that has helped many people much. It might be of use to you and to the friend whom I mentioned at the start of the chapter who found it more difficult in middle age to recover his youthful commitment to Our Lord. The story is told by a famous writer who lived in Oxford just a century after Newman and not more than four or five hundred yards from Newman's old rooms. C. S. Lewis, the great Anglican apologist, began his university career as an atheist, and his account of his conversion admirably illustrates the first two chapters in this book.

C. S. Lewis wrote:

"You must picture me alone in that room in Magdelen [College], night after night, feeling, whenever my mind lifted, even for a second, from my work, the steady, unrelenting approach of him whom I so earnestly desired not to meet. In the Trinity Term of 1929, I gave in and admitted that God was God and knelt and prayed; perhaps, that night, the most dejected and reluctant convert in all England. . . . Amiable agnostics will talk cheerfully about Man's search for God. To me, as I was then, they might as well have talked about a mouse in search of a cat."[13]

Two years later, C. S. Lewis set out for the zoo at Whipsnade in the sidecar of his friend Warren's motorbike. Lewis wrote of this journey, "When we set out, I did not believe that Jesus Christ was the Son of God and when we reached the zoo, I did."

FOUR

For us men and for our salvation
    he came down from heaven:
by the power of the Holy Spirit
    he was born of the Virgin Mary, and became man.

For our sake he was crucified under Pontius Pilate;
    he suffered, died, and was buried.
    On the third day he rose again
        in fulfillment of the Scriptures;
    he ascended into heaven
        and is seated at the right hand of the Father.
He will come again in glory to judge the living and the dead,
    and his kingdom will have no end.

Twice already in my book, I have quoted the message that Cardinal Newman gave to the university students in Dublin that "out of a careful attention to the teachings of our heart and a comparison between the claims of conscience and the announcements of the Gospel" comes the strongest argument to be had. I repeat it again now, for it seems to me all important in explaining how a Christian life evolves. Another lesson now appears that may further our understanding, though let me admit that I failed to grasp it for years. Newman tells us to compare the claims of conscience with the announcements of the Gospel, but such a comparison may also be achieved the other way around. Chronologically, conscience comes first, for we were born with it and through it we first met God. A sincere pagan, say the Emperor Marcus Aurelius, lived by conscience only; the gospel never came his way. So far, in this book, conscience was taken first, as providing the material that had to be checked. At this moment in the creed, when Our Lord becomes a man, I see that the process may be switched. Now the gospel becomes the original copy that has to be absorbed by conscience because we are moving into a situation that conscience could never have guessed. Faith is a conversation or, as Newman put it, "As prayer is the voice of man to God, so revelation is the voice of God to man."[1] The part of the creed that we now have reached belongs to Christ.

The creed appears to me as an inspiring synopsis, and its very brevity proves refreshing when we say it or sing it at Mass. Our Christian forebears certainly kept to the point. As I

60

run my eyes along my bookshelves to the various translations of the gospel and to the stout commentaries about them, I am astonished to see how the creed says everything while leaving almost everything out. No mention of the thousands of people whom Jesus met, the convoy of sick, brought from the neighborhood to be placed before him, the possessed who were freed, the sinners forgiven, the lepers cured, the thief who was promised paradise. No apostle is named in the creed, only Christ's mother and Pontius Pilate, the pagan governor who condemned him to death. All the parables and miracles, even the Sermon on the Mount, go by default. Cardinal Newman suggests that the central sacrifice of the New Covenant is missing because the early Christians protected this by secrecy. Be that as it may, the point remains valid that the creed implies much but says very little; that little nevertheless embracing everything. The one brisk statement "For us men and for our salvation he came down from heaven" expresses the whole spirit of the gospel and the one secret that conscience could not begin to guess.

The creed is a synopsis but, within its narrow framework, three short statements synopsize the creed itself. The first I have just quoted; he came down to earth for us men. The second carries the same theme of generosity further—"for our sake he was crucified under Pontius Pilate; he suffered, died, and was buried." The third, which alone looks forward to the future, tells us "his kingdom will have no end." I would like to limit my remarks to these three assertions, leaving you to select those examples from the gospel that for you best illustrate each point.

1. *For us men and for our salvation he came down
   from heaven.*

When we recall, with some care, that it is about the Living God that we are speaking, this expression of his motive for the incarnation tells us of a love that no human conscience could formulate. The inner voice of conscience tells us of God's existence, and might to someone sinless, as was his mother, also indicate his love. As we have seen, the vivid awareness of our own misconduct tends to make conscience stress our responsibility, to emphasize justice and punishment. Could God himself, with all his power, rid us of guilt without degrading our manhood by the destruction of our free will? Which one of us, even in a human court of law, would allow a plea of "diminished responsibility" to get us off the hook? Guilt is a built-in feature of each deliberate sin. We have seen fear in all forms of natural religion, the altar to the Unknown God, Virgil's version of Hell, animals and human beings as sacrificial victims for atonement, the brilliant Lucretius, who shook himself free of the gods, ending with suicide. In the Old Testament, there is fear and punishment enough for sinners, and this revealed by God himself. Prophets thundered and threatened but, as the story progresses, we see a broadening underline beneath such words as mercy, forgiveness, and hope. The psalms of King David, himself a great sinner, often speak of this. When David was old, he disobeyed God and took a census of his people for which he was allowed to choose one of three punishments. He could be harried by his enemies, suffer a famine, or suffer a pestilence. David chose pestilence and gave his reason "I am hard pressed on all sides but it is better to fall into the hands of the Lord, so rich is he in mercy, than into the hands of men."

In our permissive days, the sense of personal guilt and failure still corrodes the lives of men and women, those with religion and, still more, those with no religion, as every doctor, psychiatrist, nurse, priest, policeman, and social worker knows. It is interesting to note that John Henry Newman, a shy, reticent man, no Bible thumper in the pulpit, in his most celebrated sermons that drew the crowds in Oxford constantly reverted to this theme. This he did because he knew that men were fearful and ought to be.

The one enduring answer to fear was to come in the greatest of all God's revelations, for God so loved sinful men and women that he sent his son to pitch his tent among them, to become a man and to dwell with them on earth. At the very start of his public career with the revelation of God's sympathy for sinners not yet unfolded, Jesus said to the just but timid Pharisee Nicodemus, "God loved the world so much that he gave his only son so that everyone who believed in him may not be lost but may have eternal life." (Jn. 3:16). When we say in the creed "For us men and for our salvation" we recall just that.

No sinner in the gospel, who recognized his sin, was afraid of Jesus save only Judas, and the verdict on him must surely be "suicide while of unsound mind." Peter, little Zacheus, and the poor prostitute who wept at the dinner table were deeply sorry but never cowed. Thomas, who set conditions for his acceptance of the resurrection, was never rejected, scarcely even rebuked. The Samaritan woman with a wide assortment of husbands had her eyes opened but was so happy that she told the whole town. With Christ, really and truly God, there was no compulsion; he allowed each sinner the courtesy of taking the first step.

Leaving sinners for the moment, let us consider the fear of good people and how this was dispelled. There is a happiness in St. Luke's opening chapter not found elsewhere in the Bible, in the Old Testament or the New. Those involved were innocent and earnest, yearning for the Messiah to come but uncertain how and when God would show his hand. Their fear, though not of the guilty kind that we must suffer, hinged on the mystery of the supernatural and the majesty of the living God. Zachariah, the priest, was overcome by fear as he stood by the altar of incense in the Temple; the angel had to tell him not to be afraid. Mary was calm enough at the start of the Annunciation but became frightened when she had taken in the message; the angel said to her "Mary, do not be afraid." When she had heard the astonishing proposal that would give her a place in the creed as the Mother of God, Mary proclaimed "his mercy reaches from age to age for those who fear him" in her "Magnificat." When John the Baptist was born, his father Zachariah had recovered, and in his psalm, the "Benedictus" spoke of God releasing men from fear. We are told by St. Luke that the shepherds, tending their sheep in the fields near Bethlehem, felt "the glory of the Lord all about them" and were overwhelmed with fear. Let the angel's message to them round off this happy subject: "Do not be afraid. Listen, I bring you news of great joy, a joy to be shared by the whole people. Today, in the town of David, a savior has been born to you; he is Christ the Lord." (Lk. 2:8).

2. *For our sake he was crucified under Pontius Pilate; he suffered, died, and was buried.*

Here again, God's revelation through his only Son supports the findings of our inner conscience, for the desire to make reparation or atonement lies deep in us all. True sorrow is virtually impossible without the urge to make amends. I have never been able to forget an incident in school when I was a schoolmaster and a boy of ten who had been naughty pushed his favorite dinky car into my room. I tried to resist but suddenly knew that I had to take it, however painful it was for me. The little red car, a Jaguar, I think, had the center of my mantelpiece for three years. The donor, three years older, dropped in on occasion; he never mentioned the little red car, but he looked at it always and was pleased. Atonement is for most of us a basic need. King David saw this, in the scene just mentioned, when he chose pestilence for his punishment. God soon relented and ordered David to build an altar on Areuna's threshing floor. Once a sacrifice had been offered, the plague would cease. Areuna, the owner, when he saw the King, refused all payment; he would give the barn, the altar, and the sacrificial animals as a gift. "Nay," said David, refusing the generous offer, "I must buy it from you; the victims I offer to the Lord, my God, must not be procured without cost." (2 S. 24:10–25).

In God's revelation of himself to mankind, this desire for

64

atonement is recognized. Why, the day of Atonement was the central feast in the Hebrew calendar. The use of animals for sacrifice—no small gesture among poor, hard-working farmers, with no supermarkets around the corner—was approved and often commanded by God. Yet there was something lacking in such atonement by proxy and, after the Romans had captured and gutted the Temple, this ancient practice faded away. Strange that a universal gesture, found in almost every form of primitive religion, should, little by little, disappear.

Yet, only some forty years before the destruction of the Jewish Temple, a new sacrifice of atonement had been instituted by Christ at a Paschal supper in that upper room. Almost the whole of the Letter to the Hebrews is concerned with this astonishing change. Today some experts question whether St. Paul himself wrote this letter, but it would certainly fit in with his views. One of the key passages not only deals with the need for atonement but also shows how Christ's sacrifice differs from the old. "The blood of goats and bulls and the ashes of a heifer are sprinkled on those who have incurred defilement and they restore the holiness of their outward lives; how much more effectively the blood of Christ, who offered himself as a perfect sacrifice to God, through the eternal spirit, can purify our inner selves from dead actions so that we can do our service to the Living God." (Heb. 9:13).

For Christ to make atonement for our sins, more especially for the sin of Adam, which brought about our human downfall, he had to be a man. The question of the Fall, not explicitly mentioned in the creed, is beyond our scope on this occasion, though the flaw in ourselves is vividly seen by conscience and revealed by God in all his messages to man. What may be considered briefly here is the power gained by Christ at the incarnation that made it possible for him to make atonement because he was a man. Here we are able to see the generosity of Christ, expressed by Newman, in one of the most powerful of his Oxford sermons, as an Anglican. Newman called his sermon "The Humiliation of the Eternal Son," and

65

he preached it, if I am not mistaken, a year or so before he saw himself in the mirror "and found that I was a monophysite." I can find no trace of such a heresy here, not only no suggestion that Christ had but one nature but also a brilliant and startling description of what Christ gained by being a true man.

"After this manner then must be understood His suffering, temptation and obedience, not as if he ceased to be what he had ever been but, having clothed himself with a created essence, he made it the instrument of his humiliation; he acted in it, he obeyed and suffered through it. Do we not see among men, circumstances of a peculiar kind which throw one of our race out of himself, so that he, the same man, acts as if his usual self were not in being, and he had fresh feelings, and faculties, for the occasion, higher or lower than before? Far be it from our thoughts to parallel the incarnation of the Eternal Word with such an accidental change! I mention it, not to explain a mystery but to facilitate your conception of him who is the subject of it, to help you towards contemplating Him as God and man at once, as still the Son of God though he had assumed a nature short of his original perfection.

"That Eternal mind which, till then, had thought and acted as God, began to think and act as a man, with all man's faculties, affections and imperfections, sin excepted. Before he came on earth, he was infinitely above joy and grief, fear and anger, pain and heaviness; but afterward all these properties and many more were his as fully as they are ours. Before he came on earth, he had but the perfections of God, but, afterwards he had also the virtues of a creature, such as faith, meekness, self-denial. Before he came on earth he could not be tempted of evil but afterwards he had a man's heart, a man's tears, and a man's wants and infirmities. His Divine Nature indeed pervaded his manhood, so that every deed and word of his is in the flesh savoured of eternity and infinity; but, on the other hand, from the time he was born of the Virgin Mary, he had a natural fear of danger, a natural shrinking from pain,

66

though ever subject to the ruling influence of that Holy and Eternal Essence which was in him."[2]

The mystery remains. As Newman suggests, and this is helpful to me, we learn from Calvary, God's love for mankind and his hatred of sin. These two facts, which affect us profoundly, are not above reason or a mystery. Newman words the mystery this way: "How Christ's death expiated our sins and what satisfaction it was to God's justice are surely subjects quite above us . . . it is an event ever mysterious on account of its necessity, while it is fearful from the hatred of sin implied in it and most transporting and elevating from its display of God's love for man."[3]

To make atonement, Christ had to be one of us, a true man. But is not this once more atonement by proxy? Not for the true Christian, for the enduring tradition of the Church from apostolic times is that we unite our pains and sufferings freely to those of Christ. When an animal died in sacrifice no such sharing was possible; one may share in the suffering of a fellow man.

As Christ said, "If any man will come after me, let him deny himself, take up his cross daily, and follow me." Our atonement is expressed in that.

3. "And his kingdom will have no end."

The resurrection and ascension have been touched on in earlier chapters and may appear again in the pages that lie ahead. Under this particular heading, I would want to call your attention to Christ's quiet but overwhelming mastery. He was a gentle, unassuming man with no pretensions; if he claimed openly to be the promised Messiah and "one with the Father," such assertions made small difference to his simple life. Money, politics, heritage, publicity, and popularity played no part in his crusade. Indeed, he warned his apostles not to tell anyone about the transfiguration and hid himself once when the crowd wanted to proclaim him King. Whether the

Messiah or not, taken purely as a great historical figure, he stands unique.

Again, in the religious sphere he was, we would say, pious and observant; a devout Jew, he was often in the synagogue, a frequent pilgrim to the Temple, regular in honoring the great religious feasts. He spoke with reverence and affection of Moses and commended the Mosaic Law. He fell foul of the Establishment only when it had tampered with the law of Moses, interpreted the Mosaic Law too rigidly, and added burdens too heavy for his countrymen to bear. Even here, he respected the priestly office, and while criticizing the hypocrisy of the Elders, enjoined obedience to their authority. Christ had none of the defiance or bravado normally expected in a revolutionary. And yet, in three years—possibly only two—he effected one of the most sensational revolutions known to history.

Cardinal Newman gives us the first clue to Christ's quiet independence, a point that I would certainly have missed without Newman's help. "Though Our Lord claims to be the Messiah, he shows so little of conscious dependence on the old scriptures or of an anxiety to fulfil them, as if it became him, who was the Lord of the prophets, to take his own course and to leave their utterances to adjust themselves to him as they could and not to be careful to accommodate himself to them. The evangelists do, indeed, show some such natural zeal in his behalf and thereby illustrate what I notice in him by the contrast. They betray an earnestness to trace in his person and history the accomplishment of prophecy, as when they discern it in his return from Egypt, in his life at Nazareth, in the gentleness and tenderness of his mode of teaching and in the various, minute occurrences of his passion; but he himself goes straight on his way."[4]

Reading the gospel with the eyes of faith, believing that Christ was God incarnate, one is less surprised at the remarkable reforms that he promised and introduced. In the gospel, he appears so modest and gentle, chiefly preoccupied with the poor, the sinners, and the sick. His sermons and parables, though penetrating and disturbing, would not sweep a crowd off its feet. Yet Christ went his own way, had his own plan, a new scale of standards and values that even his own apostles could not grasp. His disciples were far more conservative, far more biblical, more concerned with national aspirations, a kingdom on earth with twelve thrones to judge the twelve tribes of Israel. Take the racial question in the Palestine of those days, a topic as devisive as anything we know today. Jews were forbidden to speak to Samaritans or to use the same cooking utensils; yet, to the astonishment of that Samaritan woman, Jesus talked to her in public and asked her for a drink. He even foretold the day when the Samaritan Temple and the Jewish Temple would pass away. Without being any less a Jew, he openly welcomed pagans and, in front of his fellow countrymen, praised the pagan centurion's greater faith. Again, he foretold the day when pagans would be the equal of the Israelites. In the Sermon on the Mount his "It was said to them of old . . . but I say to you" was a sensational advance. If we look back across the centuries to the solemnities of the two great covenants made by God with Abraham and Moses, the scene in the upper room in Jerusalem takes on an overwhelming meaning; Jesus said "Take this all of you and drink from it; this is the cup of my blood; the blood of the New and Everlasting Covenant; it will be shed for you and for all men so that sins may be forgiven."

With no wealth, no military might, no political power, no priestly office, Christ achieved all these promises. Circumcision had gone, pagans were welcome, the Temples had passed away, the new Covenant was established, sins were pardoned, and, above all, death had lost its sting.

If, toward the end of our book, we go back to recall the beginning, you will remember how, through sense, sensation, instinct, and intuition we heard the voice of conscience and knew it as the echo of God's voice. We noted at the time how conscience at first had for many of us a threatening message

69

behind which we experienced a conviction of hope. It is difficult to analyze this hope or even to attempt to word it, yet I would suggest that it was based on an intuition that the grave was not the end. It was thus for me, as a small boy, but I might well have acquired such a hope from my parents; over the years, and talking to many people, I have discovered that such a hope is widely shared. Indeed, pagans in ancient days, Virgil and Marcus Aurelius among them, also nursed this hope. St. Paul at Athens preached on the very subject, presuming that he would hold the crowd.

This sense of hope dimly experienced through conscience, mentioned or implied, though vaguely, by some Old Testament writers, is made explicit by Jesus Christ. Eternal life and the promise of it was the central theme in his crusade. He used many figures of speech, many metaphors, to convey his meaning, but the message remained the same. For the Pharisee Nicodemus, Christ used a biblical image, comparing himself to the brazen serpent that Moses had raised in the desert, "so that those who believe in him may not perish but have eternal life." (Jn. 3:14). With the Samaritan woman by the well, it was living water that would last forever; for hungry crowds in the desert it became bread that would last forever; to Martha, by her brother's grave, Jesus promised resurrection and life. His statement is worth repeating in full, for an act of faith is openly demanded: "I am the resurrection and life; he who believes in me, though he is dead, will live on, and whoever has life and has faith in me, to all eternity cannot die. Dost thou believe this?" (Jn. 11:25). His own resurrection on Easter Sunday was the final step in God's plan.

Throughout my life, I have grown in appreciation of the rare skill of the great medieval and Renaissance artists, while struggling to free myself from their physical and static concepts of the next world. The creed is free of such imagery, and for me a picture of Our Lord on a throne to the right of his Father is of little help. The escape is to return to conscience, which warned us at the start that we must face judgment; it

70

makes a great and joyful difference that the Nicene Creed should tell us our judge's name. I cannot picture Christ on a throne reigning forever, but the promise of eternal life to sinners means that "his kingdom will have no end."

FIVE

We believe in the Holy Spirit, the Lord, the giver of life,
who proceeds from the Father and the Son.
With the Father and the Son he is worshiped and
glorified.
He has spoken through the Prophets.

There are so many overtones and undertones in man's relations with the Holy Spirit that it is difficult to know where to begin. Thus, in recent decades, the West has seen a remarkable revival of the charismatic movement, which affords for its adherents a new and intuitive form of spiritual life. For these, the sensational manifestations of the first Pentecost are repeated, and the Holy Spirit assumes a dynamic force to shape their lives. The baptism of the Spirit, the gift of tongues, the powers of faith healing and other favors liberate and inspire them. We are back to the Acts of the Apostles, to the happenings in the early Church at Corinth, about which St. Paul wrote at such length.

While some are, thus, favored with such new, spiritual experiences, other Christians entertain misgivings and doubts. They ask if we may be sure that the Holy Spirit is the agent and recall similar outbursts of enthusiasm that ended in heresies and nonsense in previous centuries. I have met those who know that any such Pentecostal renovation is not for them. Yet can they be sure that such a reaction is the right one? Are they rejecting the Holy Spirit or—as I have been asked on several occasions—is the Holy Spirit rejecting them?

How fortunate it is that the Nicene Creed kept to the bare essentials and, with no trace of emotion, set out what we believe about the Holy Spirit. If we keep to the creed, whether or not we are charismatic, we cannot fool ourselves. I propose to take the three statements from the creed and to consider these briefly before moving on to other points.

1. *We believe in the Holy Spirit, the Lord, the giver
   of life.*

The last section of the previous chapter was concerned with Christ's repeated promise that he would give us eternal life. Here, in the Nicene Creed, the promise is repeated, with the Holy Spirit as the Divine agent who will accomplish this. Here was his role in the creation of the world and, in the first mention of him in the Bible, we read, "The spirit of God moved over the waters" and the world took shape. I did not mention it earlier, but we say in the creed "by the power of the Holy Spirit he was born of the Virgin Mary" so the Holy Spirit gave life to Jesus in his mother's womb. Again in the upper room in Jerusalem at Pentecost, the Spirit of God moved over the eleven apostles, and the Church came to life.

These were great occasions, but the gift of life may be found on humbler levels as well. In our contemporary world, with the theories of evolution much in favor, the action of God in nature deserves a paragraph. Monsignor Knox, with his expert knowledge of Scripture, recalls the Israelite attitude in a charming way: "I think it is quite impossible to understand the Old Testament until you see that the Jews thought of brute creation and even inanimate creation, mountains and valleys and the sun and stars and beasts and birds and fishes—they always make a great point of fishes—as conspiring to praise God all the time. And the medieval attitude was to accept that point of view about the responses of creation to God and to say 'Of course, that is the Holy Spirit; that is the response to God of nature. The love which binds the Father and the Son overflows into created things and makes them, too, aspire lovingly to God.'"[1] As a stanza from an old Victorian hymn so sweetly put it

> The monsters from the mighty deep
> Jehovah's praises shout.
> The little fish good order keep
> But wave their tails about.

75

You and I know that the Nicene Creed had in mind an activity far greater, when it named the Holy Spirit the "giver of life." Natural life, for human beings in this world, is passing; for both saint and sinner, the end is the grave. Supernatural life—that is, a life above nature—is in the gift of the Holy Spirit. A baby comes to supernatural life at Baptism. This supernatural life, which alone enables us to enjoy the bliss of heaven, was earned by Christ on Calvary and is conveyed to us by the Holy Ghost. Let me quote in full the passage, as Christ worded it to the apostles at the Last Supper, admitting that it might prove too much for them: "But when the Spirit of Truth comes he will lead you to the complete truth, since he will not be speaking as from himself but will say only what he has learned; and he will tell you all of the things to come. He will glorify me, since all he tells you will be taken from what is mine. Everything the Father has is mine; that is why I said: All he tells you will be taken from what is mine." (Jn. 16:13–15). I could well understand how anyone, taking this in, would turn charismatic, shout "Alleluia," and jump for sheer joy. But jumping for joy is a by-product; supernatural grace may be administered noiselessly and painlessly. Sometimes it is gauged only by results. The more vividly conscience makes us aware of our sinfulness and frailty, the more certain we become that an outside agent is keeping us afloat. "If I am to boast," wrote St. Paul, "then let me boast of my own feebleness," and he added Christ's personal message in prayer, "My grace is enough for you; my power is at its best in weakness."

2. *Who proceeds from the Father and the Son.*

In the previous paragraph, I quoted at length Our Lord's words to the apostles at the Last Supper so that, now, we might examine a further point. Not a few people, I find, imagine that theologians, for their own interest and occupation, create mysteries. Those who protest that they want "the religion of the heart," who seek to go straight to God, who resent

76

structured religion, as they call it, are, unwittingly, asserting that they do not want the whole truth; for the problems were not manufactured by theologians but revealed by God, the Father, often enough, through Jesus Christ. Our Lord himself admitted at the Last Supper that what he was going to tell them would, at present, be far above the apostles' heads. He went on to say that the Holy Spirit would be sent to lead them to the full truth. The creed, if you think of it carefully, is the fulfillment of that promise and a neat statement of the truth.

Cardinal Newman supplied unending inspiration to me by his skill in setting out doctrine, to pinpoint the area of mystery. One such example of his genius was given in the previous chapter, concerning Our Lord's atonement on Calvary. God's love for us and his hatred for sin are intelligible; how Christ satisfied God's justice by dying is a truth beyond our reach. Now, with the Holy Trinity, Newman clarifies our thinking and assists greatly in explaining the spirit of the creed. Earlier, I had to coin a phrase and describe Newman as "a creed man." He was precisely that. Not only does he come back to the creed again and again in his sermons and writings, but he also hammers home the point that the creed, as written, may be understood. The mysteries lie in the distance, a hundred miles beyond the foothills of the creed.

"Let it be observed," says he, "that the mystery lies, not in any one of its statements which constitute the doctrine, but in their combination. The meaning of each proposition is on the level of our understanding. There is no intellectual difficulty in approaching any one of them. God is a Father; God is a Son; God is a Holy Spirit. The Father is not the Son; The Son is not the Holy Spirit; The Holy Ghost is not the Father. God is numerically One; There are not three Gods. In which of these propositions do we not sufficiently understand what is meant to be told us? For devotion then, the mystery is no difficulty."[2] You and I are able to agree wholeheartedly to this. What is more, we lose no part of the truth if, when reciting the creed, we regard each Person of the Trinity separately. God must have intended us to do this. Otherwise, knowing our restricted vision, he would not have permitted all three Persons to appear separately at Christ's baptism.

In his *Grammar of Assent,* Newman pursues the subject further, almost to the point of mystery. In one of the most beautiful of his passages he describes it in this way: "Break a ray of light into its constituent colours; each is beautiful each may be enjoyed; attempt to unite them and perhaps you produce only a dirty white. The pure and indivisible Light is seen only by the blessed inhabitants of heaven; here we have but such faint reflections of it as its diffraction supplies; but they are sufficient for faith and devotion."[3]

This is far enough for me. In the depths of the soul or the heart or conscience, whichever one likes to call it, union with the Eternal seems to be possible. We mortals cannot, however, envisage a Being, timeless, without beginning or end. We may sense but we cannot explain or understand. So, with Monsignor Knox, we may speak of "a multiplicity of life within the Unity of the Godhead" or accept the Holy Spirit as the love between the Eternal Father and His Son. Certainly, throughout all revelation, the Holy Spirit was not only the Giver of Life, but also the Spirit of Love.

As we saw earlier, the Fathers at the Council of Nicaea were preoccupied with the safeguard of the origins, office, and dignity of God, the Son. They added a casual clause at the end of their creed, "We believe in the Holy Spirit." Fifty-six years later, at the Council of Constantinople, certain errors about the Holy Spirit were rejected; the Fathers of the Council declared that he was not created, and, hence, was not a creature but the Spirit of God. Further, the Council had to resist the theory that the Holy Spirit was the spirit of God the Father only, and not of God the Son. Both at Nicaea and at Constantinople, the traditional faith of the Church, so clearly revealed in the Scriptures, had to be defended: that there was One God but Three Persons, each with his own divine role. All three Persons were divine, and I suggest that the titles chosen by

Christ himself, while not attempting to explain a mystery far beyond our comprehension, make the link among the three Divine Persons, in human language, very plain. He told the apostles when he said adieu that they should baptize people "in the name of the Father and of the Son and of the Holy Spirit." The deep, personal bond between father and son, based on birth and heritage, is honored and understood by parents and children in this world, whether they live in Boston or Brisbane or Baltimore. Further, we human beings accept that the love of loving people cannot be contained and bottled up, inward; it breaks out and spreads to the neighborhood. Our universe is God's immediate neighborhood!

Let us be finished with the Councils of the Church. The Nicene Creed, which we recite at Sunday Mass, prefers the word "proceeds" to my word "spreads." I was thinking only of the citizens of Boston, Brisbane, and Baltimore and their loving relationships with their neighbors; the Fathers of the Council were dealing with the Holy Spirit. A person, especially a Divine Person, does not spread. He sets out with a purpose, which is love.

You and I, reared in a parliamentary, democratic system, are familiar with Acts of Parliament or Congress that are tampered with, added to, or amended and thus survive for centuries. Fifty-six years divided the Council of Nicaea from that at Constantinople, A.D. 325–81. Parliamentary, democratic systems were not known, still less talked about, in those early days. Space allows me no chance to discuss the debates, the great saints involved, or the authenticity of each assembly, but the power of the Holy Spirit may be gauged by the endurance of the Nicene Creed for rather more than fifteen hundred years.

3. *He has spoken through the prophets.*

Monsignor Knox, lecturing to his schoolgirls, found that they imagined that the Holy Spirit first intervened at Pentecost. To correct such an impression, he cited a few of the activities that I have listed—for example, the verse in Genesis that records the Spirit moving over the waters when the world began. I quoted his remarks to the children about the response to God by nature, attributed to the Holy Spirit. Two thirds of a chapter, however, is given over to the statement "He has spoken through the prophets," and Monsignor Knox switches, for the moment, from the Apostles' Creed to the Nicene to incorporate the phrase. As one who translated the entire Bible single-handed, he appreciated the assistance of the Holy Spirit and went so far as to provide a list of all the prophets, that his class might grasp how fully the Holy Spirit was engaged.[4] You and I need no such demonstration, but we are, many of us, woolly about the inspiration of the Scriptures and about prophecy.

As the Nicene Creed especially mentions the prophets, we may confine our attention to them. The word "prophet" has almost completely changed its meaning in recent centuries. Where we automatically think of a prophet as one who foretells the future, he was a preacher or seer, delivering God's message to his own people, in biblical days. The biblical prophets interest me because, throughout the Bible, they addressed their remarks to the conscience of the people, performing the functions proper to the voice of conscience in ourselves. They threatened, they insisted, they afforded some consolation and attributed much blame. The pagan religions also had their prophets, and we meet whole colonies of prophets in ancient Israel. One expert informs us that the word "prophet" means "one who is beside himself"! This much is certain, that a prophet claimed to have had direct experience of God. He was a man with a vocation, compelled to speak whether he wanted to or not. He was, therefore, charismatic, with many of the symptoms of a mystic and not a few eccentricities of his own.

There were good prophets and wicked prophets; deluded men who talked nonsense and not a few frauds. The situation has been much the same in every century among those who are "beside themselves." Yet it is through such inspired individuals that we hear the voice of the Holy Spirit. How could this be? The point to note is that a prophet spoke in the present, giving God's message to the people before him, with no clear knowledge of the future or any idea how his message would be interpreted in the centuries ahead. Thousands of such messages, no doubt, were never heard of again. Yet, centuries later, the words of Isaiah, Jeremiah, and Daniel made overwhelming sense. As the editor of *The Jerusalem Bible* puts it, "This messianic expectation runs throughout the history and sustains the faith of Israel. It was, however, expressed in terms that remained mysterious until the coming of the one who gave full realization to the prophesies and resolved their apparent contradictions in himself, i.e., Jesus, called the Christ, descended from David, born in Bethlehem, the peaceful king of Zechariah, the suffering servant of Isaiah, the child Immanuel, foretold by Isaiah, the Son of Man from the heavens, foreseen by Daniel."[5] The Holy Spirit spoke through the prophets, as the Nicene Creed says.

4. *Come O Holy Spirit, fill the hearts of thy faithful and kindle in them the fire of thy love.*

Let me use this ancient Christian invocation to the Holy Spirit to sum up his activities and our belief. His first office is to give life, as the creed tells us, and the motive for this is love. He who is the Spirit of love, between Christ and the Father, is also the supreme sign of love that they give to us. His must be the central position in my book, for this book began with the voice of conscience, our personal link with God. Though the one valid approach, conscience was not at first reassuring; with C. S. Lewis we were mice looking for a cat.

At one point in our pilgrimage we joined the Athenians, playing safe, with an extra altar to the unknown God. When St. Paul told them that this God was not unknown, that he would reveal him to them, the Athenians laughed. With Dennis and Damaris, we did not laugh but watched and listened as the greatest drama in the history of the world was unfurled. The prophets thundered and threatened, but their message grew more gentle until Christ said to Nicodemus "Yes, God so loved the world." Christ made another surprising statement to the apostles at the Last Supper: "It is better for you that I go." They must have puzzled at this, for how could it be better that he should leave them? He gave the reason "Unless I go, the Advocate will not come to you; but if I do go, I will send him to you and when he comes he will show the world how wrong it was about sin, and about what is right and about judgment." (Jn. 16:7). In some older translations, the Greek word "Paraclete" is rendered "Comforter," but this is now generally considered wrong. "Advocate" is now favored to explain the Holy Spirit's office; Monsignor Knox suggests to the children "Counsel for the Defense."

I sometimes think to myself that the Holy Spirit suffers because of the number of his gifts. Though it is true that he gives special graces for different situations, attention to them may be overdone. When I was a schoolboy, we had to learn them all by heart. The prophet Isaiah lists six, St. Paul, twelve, to which we may add the three theological virtues, faith, hope, and charity; the three sacraments, Baptism, Confirmation, and Holy Orders, plus Baptism of the Spirit, the gift of tongues and prophecy, so dear to charismatic hearts. All these gifts exist, but only spoiled children keep on thinking about presents when a very dear friend has come to stay.

This last assertion is exactly true, and the indwelling of the Holy Spirit in the hearts of the faithful is taught by the Apostles themselves. Both St. Peter and St. John refer to it, and St. Paul repeats it time and again. He speaks of this indwelling many times in the letter to the Romans and in his letters to Corinth, Ephesus, and Galatia. He writes to the Romans "People who are interested only in unspiritual things can never be pleasing to God. Your interests, however, are not in the unspiritual but in the spiritual, since the Spirit of the Son of God has made his home in you. In fact, unless you possessed

82

the Spirit of Christ you would not belong to him." (Rm. 8:9).

St. Paul conveys the intimacy between the soul and the Holy Spirit in a number of striking ways. Take this famous passage: "Everyone moved by the Spirit is a son of God. The Spirit you received is not the spirit of slaves, bringing fear into your lives again. The Spirit himself and our spirit bear united witness that we are children of God. And if we are children, we are heirs as well; heirs of God and coheirs with Christ, sharing his suffering so as to share his glory." For me the astonishment lies in the transition from the God of Conscience to the God whom I call Father; indeed, the same God but now known to be infinitely forgiving and understanding, thanks to the indwelling of the Holy Spirit.

One further passage from St. Paul to the Romans should be quoted to illustrate this intimacy. "The Spirit, too, comes to help us in our weakness. For when we cannot choose words in order to pray, properly, the Spirit himself expresses our plea in a way that could never be put into words, and God who knows everything in our hearts knows perfectly well what he means and that the pleas of the saints expressed by the Spirit are according to the mind of God." (Rm. 8:28).

Newman caps St. Paul. Where St. Paul, writing to the Ephesians (Ep. 4:30), talks of the Spirit of God marking us with his seal, Newman prefers to say that the Holy Spirit gives an earnest; a delightful old word, not much used today, but well understood in modern parlance, for an earnest is a deposit in advance. "An earnest," says Newman, "is not a mere token which will be taken away from us when it is fulfilled, as a pledge might be, but a something in advance of what is one day to be given in full." In other words, the indwelling of the Holy Spirit is not so much a pledge of heaven as a foretaste of heaven, here on earth.[6]

When Newman was vicar of St. Mary's and preached weekly, Sunday after Sunday, he drew enormous crowds. Graduates and undergraduates came in such numbers that some of the college authorities, liberal and highly suspicious of

83

the vicar, shifted the time of lunch in college in an effort to keep people away. As his audience was made up of earnest listeners, the preacher set a high standard, especially when he spoke about the indwelling of the Holy Spirit in the soul of man. Time and again, he made the distinction between what was outward and what was inward; circumcision for the Israelites outward, baptism for the Christian inward; the brazen serpent, raised by Moses, outward; inward, the atonement made by Christ on the Cross. The indwelling of the Holy Spirit required for Newman a change in the inward man.

It is for this reason that I bring in Newman to end this chapter, for he, more than any other, stressed that our lives should be different, that Christianity implied much more than keeping out of sin. "This," he said, "was more an absence than a presence, the presence of the Holy Trinity, the Living God." One sentence in particular struck me: "We are like those persons who perhaps have never fallen into gross sin and yet live a life of ease and indolence as far as they can—or, at least, who, far from setting the glory of God before them, as the end of their being, live for themselves, not for God. And what especially lulls their consciences in so doing, is the circumstance that they have never sinned grossly or are not sinning grossly; forgetting that a mirror is by nothing more commonly dimmed than by the small and gradual accumulations of daily impurities and that souls may silently be overspread and choked up by mere dust until they reflect back no portion of the heavenly truth which should possess them."[7]

SIX

We believe in one holy catholic and apostolic Church.

Many of us have known the creed since childhood; we must have recited it thousands of times across the years. The words have not changed since A.D. 400, but the emphasis has altered; the creed that I sang, as a treble, in our school choir is not quite the same as the one I croak today. St. Paul put his finger on the point of difference when he wrote to the Corinthians "When I was a child, I talked like a child, had the thoughts of a child; since I became a man, I have outgrown childish ways." (1 Co. 13:11). One of the predominant traits of childhood, as I saw as a schoolmaster, is to be prejudiced and partisan. For the majority of teen-agers there is a constant refrain that my class, my school, my team, my girl, my country "is the best ever," to which, as a roaring Roman Catholic, I added, "my Church." I very much hope that readers from other denominations were as prejudiced as I was; as a boy in downtown London, I rarely passed a church of another persuasion without thanking God that I was not a Protestant!

Such an attitude was seen as a virtue in my boyhood; when you come to think of it, young Saul thought he was doing right when he persecuted the first Christians as an up-and-coming Pharisee. Though he deeply regretted the past, including his part in the stoning of St. Stephen, he never admitted this as a sin. Nor need we. Long ago, in Devonshire, we children were shut in a back room of a Sunday morning that we might not so much as see the local parson as he walked across the drive in his surplice to conduct the Communion service in the local church. As you will have guessed, I managed to glimpse him

86

and, later, duly confessed "I saw the parson" to the astonishment of an Irish priest on the other side of the grille. Both sides were as earnest and as mad. An old, old man told me, long ago, how, on his way to school in London, his parents made him promise to sprint past that wicked building, the Brompton Oratory. The promise was broken, the sprint grew slower and slower, and the same boy ended up as an old, old Jesuit.

In the days when I sang the creed as a child, this article about the one holy catholic and apostolic Church caused me no problems and was the one that I liked the best. I sang it louder than the rest. The articles concerning the birth, death, and resurrection of Our Lord were easy, as I could picture him. On the mantelpiece in my bedroom, I had my favorite statues, St. Joseph in green, Our Lady in blue and with a rapt expression, Jesus in white and red. That various Protestant aunts regarded my statues as blasphemy, veering toward idolatry, proved an effective stimulus to prayer. The creed tapered away for me after that, for I could not picture God the Father and though, as a devout child I duly saluted the Holy Spirit, I could not bring myself to pray to a sanctified dove!

Over the decades, in a gradual process, the creed has turned upside down. Thanks very much to John Henry Newman and his views on conscience, the three Persons of the Holy Trinity are now experienced. Freed from imaginings and reached by sense, sensation, instinct, and intuition, their existence has become real to me and they themselves are twice as large as life. Yet, with the waning of imagination, the gospel story is losing some of its glorious color, perhaps more challenging in black and white. It is, however, belief in the Church that, for me, has altered most. This has happened in three ways. First, where all the other articles of the creed are now fixed and changeless, the Church, because it is both divine and human, is, in one sense, a contradiction, part changeless, part liable to change. Next, this article used to seem easy and less important, hooked on at the end of the creed after Father, Son, and

Holy Spirit. Now it has ceased to be peripheral and occupies the very center of the stage. Were we to ask ourselves what was the motive of Father, Son, and Holy Spirit in initiating the long drama of the incarnation, we might answer that God wanted to give us hope, faith, and atonement, but all these add up to one answer: He wanted to found the Church. Third, this article of the creed is the only one that we, in the twentieth century, are able to do anything about. With all the others, we just believe and express our thanks. The Church is our concern as once it was the concern of St. Paul, St. Athanasius, St. Leo, and the others mentioned in each chapter, including Cardinal Newman and Monsignor Knox. The creed itself grows more precious as it gets older, as the distances lengthen, landmarks vanish, and the centuries scurry away.

I do not propose to comment on all the four statements included in this article. The article itself seems to have been added to the creed in the fourth century, but the four adjectives, one, holy, catholic, and apostolic were used by themselves much earlier. Thus the key word "catholic" first appears in the time of St. Ignatius of Antioch, the disciple of St. Peter and of St. Polycarp, trained by St. John.

1. *We believe in the Church.*

The very first Christians, after Pentecost, huddled together in Jerusalem, would hardly have troubled to say that the Church was one. They knew it was holy, for the Holy Spirit had just descended on them; it was not catholic when confined to Palestine. There was, finally, no need to proclaim it apostolic with Peter, James, John, and the other apostles writing letters and busying about. The first act of faith for them, and for us, must be in the Church itself.

They were more fortunate than we are in that they never knew the ugly and vague word "Church." Experts still argue about its origin and derivation, and the English-speaking peoples treat it carelessly. The Church may be a building, a synod of clergymen, an institution, or the six members of the latest sect. In the Greek of those early days and, later, in Latin, the word used was *ecclesia*. *Ecclesia* meant an assembly of people with a common purpose; Monsignor Knox informed his schoolgirls that the ancient Athenians called their House of Commons the *ecclesia*.

The all-important point about the first Christians was that they made an open commitment to an assembly established for a purpose by Jesus Christ, Our Lord. How far they appreciated in advance what was going to happen we have no means of knowing, but there was nothing haphazard at the start. Christ had often spoken about the Church in his lifetime, as often as not calling it the Kingdom of God. He had picked St. Peter to be the leader and had established a new covenant at the Last Supper, one which was to be repeated in his memory. Before he ascended to heaven, he gave the apostles their commission to make disciples of all nations and they, further, received the power to forgive sins. They certainly were told that he would be leaving shortly but that he would send his spirit as their Advocate. What they made of all this we may never know, but at least they obeyed his last commandment, to go back to Jerusalem and wait. They retired to the upper room with Mary his mother, and they prayed.

At Pentecost, the pieces of the puzzle fell into place. I have often come across a sentimental and erroneous image of the earliest Christians as starry-eyed, simple people, free of all structure, spouting extempore psalms from the love in their hearts. Yet the Acts of the Apostles, our only record of what happened, bristles with American efficiency. The immediate election of St. Matthias to replace Judas was extraordinary; did Christ leave any instructions about this? Small assemblies were set up for prayers in the Temple and for the "breaking of bread." Then we have the appointment of seven deacons; funds were organized, alms distributed, not without a little trouble, and Barnabas was practical enough to sell a plot of land to assist the cause. From the very first, the apostles commissioned those who would spread the good news. It was, early, decided to approach the Israelites first. From St. Luke's account, the Council of Jerusalem was conducted efficiently by men with little previous experience, four of them fishermen. On one subject only was there some confusion, the Second Coming of Our Lord. A few, including one or two of the apostles, expected it immediately; not all, for plans were made to approach the pagan world. This mission to the Gentiles, conducted chiefly by Barnabas and Paul, was a bold, startling decision, a break with Jewish traditional thinking, led by one who described himself as "a Pharisee of Pharisees."

The significance of these first steps in the growth of the infant Church lies in the acceptance by the apostles that the Church was to be the extension of Christ's life on earth. The incarnation was not planned for the spiritual benefit of those only who chanced to be alive and living in Palestine at one particular point of time. Christ had died for all mankind. Though their horizon at the start was no farther away than Asia Minor, the apostolic vision was already universal in theory; they knew that Christ died for mankind all the world over and that he would be with the Church to the end of time.

The early Christians never pictured the Church as a building but as an assembly of many peoples with a common purpose, to spread the good news to all. As devout Jews, one such assembly satisfied their deepest aspirations, the long, wearisome trek of the Chosen People from Egypt to the Promised Land. They saw the continuity. The pattern of divine thought revealed in the Old Testament story was being repeated by Christ in the New. As with Moses, long ago, their pilgrimage began with a new convenant, a Passover supper, a Paschal lamb. They had their manna, their brazen serpent, and, with the promise of the Holy Spirit, a pillar of fire by night. We need to appreciate this to understand the letters of the Apostles, especially the ardent letters of St. Paul. If the ancient Jewish imagery means less to some of us now, the Christian repetition of the pilgrimage made by Moses tells us much about the mind of God. I find for myself that any effort is worthwhile to acquire the habit of picturing the Church as a pilgrimage. We have no familiar landmarks, a constantly changing background, but the common purpose, the same good companions, and the same good news. *Gulliver's Travels,* the *Canterbury Tales,* and *Pilgrim's Progress* retain their freshness by this very device. If you are holy and need Scriptural support, why not fall back on Our Lord himself and on his ancestor, King David, both of whom saw a good shepherd leading his sheep to pastures new? The recent General Council of the Church, Vatican II, was moved to stress this ancient and all-rewarding image of the Church.

2. *We believe in* one *Church.*

The need to stress the unity of the Church was not felt at Pentecost, but by Chapter 5 of the Acts of the Apostles, Ananias and Sapphira had paid a grim penalty, not available to bishops, today. In connivance, they had kept back certain monies and, as St. Peter put it, "lied to the Holy Spirit." (Ac. 5:1). In the very next chapter of the Acts, Greek and Jewish factions in Jerusalem were squabbling about the Widows' Fund. (Ac. 6:1). St. Stephen was still alive, young Saul from Tarsus was in the city as a student and, at a guess, the Holy Spirit had come down on the apostles "in recent months."

I mention these sad events to correct a widespread but dangerous impression that all the early Christians were saints. We have here a malicious, diabolical rumor that has done untold damage throughout history. Every red-hot reformer, Catholic or Protestant, has chastised the decadence of his contemporary society and pointed a condemning forefinger to the pure, simple, "praise God" standards of early Christian days. Monsignor Ronald Knox, who translated the Bible and taught catechism to schoolgirls, traced this evil boosting of the presumed virtue of early Christians through every period of Church history.

91

He wrote in his admirable book *Enthusiasm:* "It is a common assumption, bred in our minds by pious literature and frequent pulpit denunciations that the first age of the Church was, in every respect, a golden age. So it has appeared, especially, to leaders of later, enthusiastic movements. Your prophet, who passes for an innovator in the eyes of his contemporaries, does not admit the charge; he claims, rather, to be restoring the godly discipline which flourished in apostolic times, now overgrown with neglect. . . . Do we really find perfect harmony, severe moral standards, unquestioned loyalty to the apostolic teaching evinced everywhere among the rank and files of Christendom? Is there not rather reason to suspect that, in those early days, error followed hard on the heels of truth and liberty would not have been slow, but for incessant vigilance, to degenerate into licence?"[1]

Monsignor Knox was right in raising his last questions, to both of which his book supplies the answer "Yes." The early Christians set out with enthusiasm and high endeavour and died heroically in their thousands when the Roman persecutions began. But, filled with the Holy Spirit as they were, they still were human, as good and as bad as the Christians of today. The moral for us is vigilance or, as Christ so often put it, "watch and pray."

Peter, James, Jude, and John, of the original twelve apostles, wrote to the faithful burning words of warning; Peter sent this message "As there were false prophets in the past history of our people, so, you too, will have your false teachers, who will insinuate their own disruptive views and disown the Master who purchased their freedom." (2 P. 2:1). St. Jude adds a further point: "My dear friends, remember what the apostles of Our Lord Jesus Christ told you to expect. At the end of time, they told you, there were going to be people who sneer at religion and follow nothing but their own desires for wickedness. These unspiritual and selfish people are nothing but mischiefmakers." (Jude 1:17).

St. Paul, as always, suffered in person from these attacks.

He had come to Corinth toward the end of A.D. 50 and remained in that city for eighteen months. When he moved on to Ephesus in A.D. 52, he left behind in Corinth a small but enthusiastic Christian community. Perhaps, a year later, three Corinthians made the tedious journey to Ephesus, to pour out their woes to their beloved Paul. The Christian community in Corinth was falling to pieces due to factions, false prophets, immorality, and cliques. There were abuses at the holy sacrifice, Christians washing their dirty linen in public, and charismatics rivaling each other in speaking in tongues. Some, self-appointed prophets, were challenging St. Paul's authority.

Of course, he coped. But he began his first extant letter to the Corinthians with two highly embarrassing questions to the rival factions: "What, I mean, are all these slogans?" and "Has Christ been parceled out?" Every line of both these letters to the Corinthians deserves attention, for the rivalries and feuds in the Christian community at Corinth would be repeated, century by century, throughout the long history of the Church. Moses and Paul faced much the same problems on their pilgrimage.

In the thirteenth chapter of his first letter to Corinth, Paul wrote his famous passage about charity, one of the most beautiful, surely, in all religious literature. Phrases that would inspire the saints in later ages brought only blushes to many a Corinthian face. This most expressive description of charity ever written was mailed to Christians eaten up with uncharity. If we miss the secret sarcasm of the opening paragraph, we may also miss the point "I may speak with every tongue which men and angels use; yet, if I lack charity, I am no better than echoing bronze, or the clash of cymbals. I may have powers of prophecy, no secret hidden from me, no knowledge too deep for me; I may have utter faith, so that I can move mountains; yet, if I lack charity, I count for nothing." (1 Co. 13).

When we say "We believe in one Church" we commit ourselves to one faith, one hope, but, above all, to the virtue of Christian charity.

3. *We believe in one holy* catholic *Church.*

As I have said already, the word "catholic" came into use in the days of St. Ignatius and St. Polycarp. It was a common Greek word meaning universal; the Greeks had another word with much the same meaning—"ecumenical"—which has been translated as "all over the civilized world." As far as is known, "catholic" was first introduced to distinguish the Church as a whole from the local communities springing up in Alexandria, Corinth, and Antioch. By the fourth century, when it was added to the creed, "catholic" had acquired a wider connotation as the frontiers of Christianity spread. At the same time, "ecumenical" was used for the General Councils; Nicaea was the first Ecumenical Council of the Church.

When the first Christians called themselves Catholics, they did not intend to imply that the Church was in every part of the world. In fact, it was not. At that period, the Catholic Church was largely confined to Asia Minor, but with outposts and small beginnings in Spain and Rome. While the Roman Empire was still pagan and Christianity proscribed and persecuted, growth was more slow. With the conversion of the Emperor Constantine, a period of great missionary endeavor carried the faith to much of the known Western world. The word "catholic" implied that the Christian Church was designed for all peoples, all the world over, was not parochial, provincial, racist, or elite.

Two approaches to the title Catholic may be suggested here. The first comes from Cardinal Newman on a historic occasion, when the first London Oratory was opened on King William Street, off the Strand. Newman came from Birmingham to preach one of the first of his sermons as a Catholic. He took an unusual view of Catholicism but one that is helpful in restless times. He said of the Church, "She has passed through the full cycles of changes, in order to show us that she is independent of them all. She has had trial of East and West, of monarchy and democracy, of peace and war, of imperial and feudal tyranny, of times of darkness and times of philosophy, of bar-

barousness and luxury, of slaves and freemen, of cities and nations, of marts of commerce and seats of manufacture, of old countries and young, of metropolis and colonies." As I hurry through history, seeking examples for each of Newman's statements, I piece together a delightful picture of Catholicity.[2]

The second approach to the label Catholic—it is more like a lesson—was taught in the recent General Council of the Church. Previous General Councils had been restricted very largely to Europe; difficulties of travel had excluded almost all the bishops from the New World. As the Catholicism of the early Church came near to becoming limited to the eastern Mediterranean, so in our lifetime, Europe was the faith. When Hilaire Belloc coined this slogan, he saw it as a compliment. The Second Council of the Vatican could not regard it in this light. Thanks to easy air travel, three thousand bishops could make the journey, many of them from countries that had never been represented at a General Council before. The frontiers of the Church had been enormously extended, and Catholic took on a meaning far deeper than the world of my boyhood could have guessed.

Was the Church prepared for such a growth? Europe had been the faith. For many, many centuries, the Popes had been European, mainly French and Italian. To stand much chance of canonization, a holy man had to be in easy spitting distance of the Mediterranean. The heroic missionaries—and they were heroic—carried the French, Spanish, German, and English cultures across continents. At a great Indian Congress, with many thousands of Hindus present, a hymn from the Westminster Cathedral hymnal was sung. As Latin was still in use, young men in Africa or Asia, yearning for the priesthood, had this heavy burden imposed.

At the second Vatican Council, one sensed the Holy Spirit present and very much at work. In language, and liturgy, music, culture, and custom, the Fathers gave a new dimension to the proud title of the Catholic Church.

As I said earlier, the other articles of the creed are now

changeless; this article alone demands of us action as well as faith. When we say "We believe in one holy catholic Church," we commit ourselves to a right attitude in many modern problems, racialism, culture, and the poorer regions of our world.

4. *We believe in one holy catholic and apostolic Church.*

God's use of men as apostles is as old as the Bible itself. An apostle is one who is sent by God on a special mission, and the patriarch Joseph told his frightened brethren that God had sent him into Egypt to make plans that the family might survive. (Gn. 45:6–8). Moses, straight from the burning bush, was sent on a mission to Pharaoh "to bring the sons of Israel, my people out of Egypt" (Ex. 3:10), and there are countless other examples of men being used by God in this way. We also have an example of men being punished because, though not so commissioned, they undertook a project by themselves. Jeremiah reports "Then Yahweh said to me, 'The prophets are prophesying lies in my name; I have not sent them, I gave them no orders, I never spoke to them'." These prophets would be punished for proclaiming "daydreams of their own." (Jr. 14:14).

In the New Testament, Our Lord himself is once called an apostle by St. Paul. Certainly, Jesus was commissioned by God, the Father, to redeem the world. Jesus commissioned apostles in his turn. He spent a whole night in prayer before he chose the twelve; he gave them careful training, much enlightenment, and official status "He that receives you, receives me, and he that receives me receives Him who sent me." (Mt. 10:40). He added later "No one knows the Father except the Son and those to whom the Son chooses to reveal him." (Mt. 11:25).

The apostles, then, enjoyed a unique and overwhelming honor and responsibility. Ordinary sinful men, they were chosen to play a part in the revelation of God's plans. They were to be the human link between the three Persons of the Holy Trinity and mankind. Let me repeat once more the final com-

96

mission that they received from Christ on ascension day: "All authority in heaven and on earth has been given to me. Go, therefore, make disciples of all nations, baptising them in the name of the Father and of the Son and of the Holy Spirit, and teach them to observe all the commands I gave you. And know that I am with you always, yes, even to the end of time." (Mt. 28:18).

When we say "We believe in one holy catholic and apostolic Church" we have before us Christ's final commission to the eleven apostles and make an act of faith in that. We accept all authority, not only in heaven but also on earth. On Christ's authority, the apostles carried baptism and a new life into this world. Their commission gave them the authority to teach the true doctrine that they had had from Christ. They were to govern the Church with Christ protecting them until the end of time.

They are said, traditionally, to have remained in Jerusalem and Palestine for twelve years. They then scattered to carry out their commission in every part of the known world. Records were few and, though we treasure traditions about them, some of the twelve vanish from view. With others, many more details have survived. In their letters, as we have seen, they often warned the faithful against false doctrines and innovations; all that we know of St. Peter, St. Paul, St. John, St. Jude, and St. James shows them to be utterly loyal to Christ's teaching, strictly orthodox and conservative. When evidence appears to show how they handed on their commission to others, we are compelled to believe that they understood Christ's mandate in that way. St. Paul's letters to Timothy and Titus give us clear indications and St. Clement, St. Peter's disciple, writes in a letter to Corinth "For this reason [the likelihood of contention], the apostles exercised proper forethought and appointed the aforesaid and, afterward, they imposed an additional law that if these should go to their rest, other tested men should have the succession to their ministry." This is not the place to do justice to the evidence. Sufficient to note that in the century following the deaths of the apostles, their sacramental and teaching commissions were handed on.

The lesson for us, surely, is found in acceptance wholeheartedly of the authority of the Church. Ages vary, but we live at a time when authority in government, family life, industry, and law and order is under attack. When we look at the Church and recall the long story of God's revelation, the promises made, the price paid by Christ, and the love he showed us, we ourselves would want to live under his authority. The voice of conscience itself, more than historic evidence, tells me that where God is, there also is authority. As Paul wrote to Timothy, "Timothy my son, these are the instructions that I am giving you; I ask you to remember the words once spoken over you by the prophets and taking them to heart, to fight like a good soldier with faith and good conscience for your weapons. Some people have put conscience aside and wrecked their faith in consequence." (1 Tm. 18).

5. *The last word.*

I saw no reason to detain you on the word "holy" in the Nicene Creed's description of the Church. Though the Church was established for the sake of mankind, both for saints and for sinners, the means that she offered us, the sacraments, grace, the indwelling of the Holy Spirit, all help to strengthen our good resolves.

The creed does not mention the Pope in person, so there is a hot potato that I might reasonably leave in the pot. At the time of Nicaea, the Pope was out of the catacombs and dwelling in Imperial Rome. He sent two representatives to the Council but did not make the journey himself. As the successor of St. Peter, he is covered in the creed by the apostolic nature of the Church.

At the end of this chapter, let the first Pope have the last word. In his second epistle to the Christians living among pagans in Pontus, Galatia, and Cappadocia, St. Peter makes a capital point. He writes "But there is one thing, my friends, that you must never forget; that, with the Lord, a day can mean a thousand years and a thousand years is like a day. The Lord is not being slow to carry out his promises, as anyone else might be called slow; but he is patient with all, wanting nobody to be lost and everybody be brought to change his ways."

Though Peter is writing to those who were impatient about Christ's second coming, the lesson that he teaches remains true and as compelling now. An irresistible urge in us all makes us impatient if things are not brought to fruition at once and in our own day. God is timeless and, as Peter reminds us, a day for Him might mean a thousand years. Let me try to illustrate the point. We used to pray earnestly for the conversion of Russia, a Christian state, now officially atheist for some sixty years. Nothing happened, and we felt that our prayers had not been heard. What is sixty years to God? The brutal Roman persecutions of the early Church lasted for two hundred years and, then, quietly, without warning, the Emperor was converted and the Fathers turned up at Nicaea, not much the worse for wear. Again, after not much more than fifty years of work by a handful, we grow impatient that the cause of reunion seems to take so long. Yet the various branches of Arianism divided Christendom for centuries and now look trivial from far away.

Were God to act in haste, mankind would be the loser, as St. Peter says. Each instant confrontation appears to us as a crisis, especially in our own times and to us, who are media men. One smiles now to look back to controversies that almost divided Europe but mean nothing to us today. That phrase in the Nicene Creed "one in Being with the Father" once had devout theologians at each other's throats. Another article of the creed, "who proceeds from the Father and the Son," almost caused a rift between East and West. St. Gregory Nazianzen, Doctor of the Church, who agreed with the doctrine, pleaded for caution and urged that it should not be told to everyone. Few miss a moment's sleep, today, over the *filioque* clause. An example nearer home is the word "transubstantiation," a red rag to the Protestant protagonists of the sixteenth-century Reformation world. Catholic priests and laymen laid down their lives for that word while, because of it, the English Establishment declared the Mass an idolatrous sacrifice. Today, especially at ecumenical gatherings, many non-Catholics love to attend Mass.

I certainly do not intend to maintain that such controversies were trivial; no, they were earnest and important, but God takes his time, and the pilgrim Church moves on. A century ago, no writer would have written or staged the play *A Man for All Seasons,* and twenty-five years ago the discarding of Latin by the Catholic Church after so many centuries would have been judged unthinkable. One has to smile. No Protestant in Victorian times would have touched the Douai Bible; no fervent Catholic, in a court of law, would have taken an oath on the Bible unless a copy of the Douai was dusted and produced. Today, we have some eight new translations of the Bible, some Protestant, others Catholic, and a few mixed!

These extraordinary shifts of opinion are made possible because God acts slowly; a day for him can mean a thousand years. Some previous contentions disappear and new ones are created, as when politicians, of no clear religious belief, and for other motives, legalize abortion; or scientists, after what the journalists herald as a breakthrough, market the very latest contraceptive pill. I wonder what people, a century from now, will make of our troubles or what will have happened to the vexed question of women priests? We must keep our cool as did Moses in the desert and face each pestilence or discontent as it comes. All said and done, Newman's suggestion of checking conscience against the teachings of the gospel stands one in good stead. If, for God, a day can be a thousand years, then the Nicene Creed is barely two days old!

This is an amusing world. Out here, on the islands where I live, we three ministers of religion try to meet weekly to pray together and to intercede for our flocks. Such a pious and delightful exercise could not have happened twenty-five years ago. Today we are more than bosom friends. Each Tuesday morning, I set out to walk for five minutes either to the Methodist Church House or to the Anglican Rectory. This is not the whole story, for, on the third Tuesday, my colleagues walk for five minutes in the other direction to pray with me. On that special morning, I am up early to clean the carpet and to hide the ashtrays. We recite the Anglican Morning Prayers, a new exercise in a Jesuit presbytery. We use the Coverdale version of the psalms, for me a slight embarrassment, for, over my mantelpiece, in the place of honor, hangs Holbein's sketch of St. Thomas More. Now, More had no love for Coverdale and laid down his life on the other side. I sometimes wonder, when we pray for the Queen what Mary Queen of Scots is thinking; I have a melancholy Victorian watercolor of this hapless soul on her way to the scaffold and face it at every meal. I have yet to tell my colleagues that, on my bedroom door, is Henry VIII in a brass doorknocker; I bang his head with great pleasure every night!

Yet I love our weekly prayer meetings and the real sense of unity that they bring. I must, however, admit that I was distracted, once, in the middle of a psalm, my mind drawn to the portrait on the wall opposite; there was old Cardinal Newman, in his day evangelical, Anglican, and Roman Catholic, watching us!

EPILOGUE

We look for the resurrection of the dead
and the life of the world to come.

As life ebbs away and the old move gently toward the later sixties, a deep and enduring satisfaction sometimes cushions their descent. Not all, alas, find this inward peace. Some fear old age, others resent it; it has cast long shadows across their lives for many years. When the last camouflage has failed and the facts of life may no more be papered over, some sad old people lapse into apathy. They revert to the ploys that worked in childhood: sulking, self-pity and peevishness.

Part of such depression may be physical. The soul is also involved, and we should heed the warnings of the great American psychologist, William James. James wrote "a naturalistic view of life, however enthusiastically it may begin, is sure to end in sadness; this sadness is at the very heart of every agnostic, naturalistic philosophy." George Orwell put the same another way. In a learned journal, many years ago, he discussed epitaphs, those amusing, here-lies-the-body-of verses and inscriptions found in the old churchyards of Britain and North America. After making his readers laugh, Orwell suddenly inserted a line of dots, beneath which he posed a telling question: "Why do we not have funny epitaphs today?" His answer was exact: "Now that people no longer believe in another world, death is no longer a funny subject!"

George Orwell was right, and death for many today is the ultimate, the final cul-de-sac. William James, too, does us a favor by stressing the unhappiness that inevitably follows for those who have reached the wrong answers and thus missed the point of life. Yet you and I have known hundreds of cheerful and hopeful men and women who found more happiness in the autumn of life than they ever knew in the spring. This is not to suggest that they were unhappy in childhood but that, now, in old age, they have discovered this deep and enduring satisfaction that breaks the time barrier and provides a foretaste of eternity. My mother was one of these. As a widow of seventy-four, living alone, she once assured me that she had never been so happy; I smiled, but cynically. Now, at sixty-seven myself, I rehearse the apologies that she is sure to expect!

Such a deep and abiding satisfaction stems from faith. It is entirely free of all smugness and complacency. One may be wholly satisfied with life and yet equally dissatisfied with one's own performance and with the wasted years. This inner joy derives from no sense of personal achievement, however valid or even praiseworthy this may be. A man should be proud if he has made good in his field, if he has climbed the ladder and gained a reputation with matching salary. He should exult in a happy home, in a daughter doing brilliantly at college, in a son whom everyone says takes after him. Yet, despite such achievements, he may still feel dissatisfaction and emptiness. When it comes to medical checks, a lump near the ribs, a hint about major surgery, it is small consolation to know that you may die as vice president of a flourishing textile company.

The only deep and enduring satisfaction comes from a real —not a notional—assent to the life beyond the grave. In the creed we say "We look for the resurrection of the dead," and we must do just this. My book ends where it began, with the voice of conscience, a voice so very much more gentle for those who have grasped God's love for them.

A slim paperback with an engaging title has helped me greatly in the past eight years. The book is called *Man's Search for Meaning;* the author is Dr. Viktor Frankl, an Austrian psychotherapist of international repute. Space permits no full summary here, beyond the blurb on the cover, which I fully endorse. "Is there any meaning to life; in death, in suffering, in work, in sex, in love? How can a sense of meaning help secure mental health? What is the role of the doctor in conveying this meaning?" These are the questions confronted by Dr. Frankl, world-famous psychiatrist and leading proponent of existential analysis. Drawing on his vast store of case histories as well as on his personal experience as an inmate of Nazi concentration camps, Dr. Frankl presents a brilliant antidote to the inner emptiness and purposelessness that have become the mass neurosis of the century.[1]

An experienced and an increasingly religious man, Dr. Frankl recalls from his agonizing years in Auschwitz a striking and never-to-be-forgotten fact. After his release he wrote, "In spite of all the enforced physical and mental primitiveness of life in a concentration camp, it was possible for the spiritual life to deepen. Sensitive people, who were used to a rich, intellectual life, may have suffered much pain (they were often of a delicate constitution), but the damage to their inner selves was less. They were able to retreat from their terrible surroundings to a life of inner riches and spiritual freedom. Only in this way, can one explain the apparent paradox that some prisoners, of less hardy makeup, often seemed to survive camp life better than did those of a robust nature."

Dr. Frankl names his book *Man's Search for Meaning,* but I would like to change this to *Man's Search for Faith.* Faith, when you come to think of it, is that fuller meaning that enabled the religious prisoners to survive the barbarities of the concentration camp. For us, who accept the creed, life acquires this fuller meaning, an experience, especially true, in our approach to death. Any human being who sincerely says "I look for the resurrection" will never know a useless or purposeless moment, right up to his or her last breath.

A notional, generalized assent to a vague life hereafter is not sufficient to provide the fuller meaning to life on earth. We must go back to Newman's assertion "I am as little able to think with any mind but my own as to breathe with another's lungs." We have to repeat the full exercise again and to climb up through sense, sensation, instinct, and intuition to reach a personal and real assent to life after death. The effort is not great. As we saw in the gospel, when Christ spoke of eternal life to Martha, to the Samaritan woman, to Nicodemus, and to others, the response was immediate, especially from Martha, with her brother lying dead. Newman wrote on the death of his father, "On Thursday, he looked beautiful, such calmness, sweetness, composure and majesty were in his countenance. Can a man be a materialist who sees a dead body? I had never seen one before."

There exists a wide difference between seeing the dead body of a much-loved person and imagining the life after death. I derive no help, no strengthening of faith, no fuller meaning, from pictorial efforts to create Heaven or Hell. Even masterpieces by some of the world's greatest artists, perfectly executed, not only fail to assist me but also appear to damage my faith. If I am unable to think with a mind not my own, neither can I see with eyes not my own. The visions described by St. John in the Revelation leave me cold. Each for himself. How picture the resurrection of the dead, the last Trump, the frantic search for missing members; those who were cremated in a piteous state? Nor does it make me yearn for heaven to inspect representations of eternal bliss. Who wants to see the Lamb of God standing on an altar, mitered bishops swinging censers, angels playing their ukeleles, with "hallelujahs" ringing in the vaults above? The heaven of the spirituals is no more attractive with everlasting cigars and Louis Armstrong tootling in the background; I loved Louis Armstrong, but the thought of jazz for eternity might make some of us think that we had come to the wrong address. Fooling apart, imagination rarely provokes a real assent.

If, as I suggest, faith is not only a search for meaning but also the discovery of meaning, then it must be based on facts. The creed for us provides those facts. We move from the altar to the unknown God to meet the God who was known by Abraham and Moses; whose plans were anticipated by the prophets; whose Son became a man and was identified by John the Baptist, the greatest of the prophets; the Son "who for us men and for our salvation" laid down his life. We rub our eyes when we hear the promise of eternal life and of his Spirit given as an earnest for such a life.

I plan, in the last pages of my book, to suggest, in the lives of three or four remarkable people, how belief in the resurrection of the dead works out. First, however, let us pause to watch Holy Simeon, one of the most charming figures in the gospel story, mentioned only by St. Luke. (Lk. 2:25).

Luke tells his story in four sentences: 1. "At this time, there was a man, named Simeon, living in Jerusalem, an upright man of careful observance who waited patiently for comfort to be brought to Israel." Simeon's faith began blind. He trusted but had no way of knowing how and when such comfort would come. At least he was patient, and we might copy him in that. 2. "By the Holy Spirit, it had been revealed to him that he was not to meet death until he had seen the Christ whom the Lord anointed." Though we cannot compare ourselves with Simeon in holiness or careful observance, we enjoy with him one considerable gift in common, the indwelling of the Holy Spirit. 3. "He now came, led by the Spirit into the temple and, when the child Jesus was brought in by his parents, to perform the customs which the law enjoined concerning him, Simeon, too, was able to take him in his arms." At this point, Simeon had what I must call an "experience," for want of a better word. Nothing in St. Luke's account suggests that the poor young couple with their baby son were outstanding or exceptional. Their boy would not hit the headlines for another thirty years. Yet Simeon, suddenly, found certainty. 4. His short but majestic psalm, the *Nunc Dimittis,* may be rendered loosely "At last my eyes have seen salvation and I am happy to die."

It would be impudent to compare ourselves to Simeon and I would, also, be dishonest if I gave the impression that I had a hot line to the Holy Spirit. The example that helps me is the

108

opposite of charismatic; it is down-to-earth and within our competence. I was never gifted at mathematics and maybe for this reason few puzzles have ever attracted me. I have, however, noticed with crossword fiends, chess competitors, patience addicts, and jigsaw puzzlers that, after hours, even days, of complete frustration, they suddenly spotted the true solution in a flash. Up to that moment they had been guessing, assuming, chasing red herrings, even cheating, just a little, to squeeze an answer out. With the room in a mess, tempers frayed, channels blocked, counters deadlocked, ashtrays full, promises empty, someone, somehow, somewhere saw the truth. He or she may have been staring at the board, woken up at night, may have left the overheated room in desperation and volunteered to take the dog for a walk. Between lamp-post and tree, the clues, counters, cards fell into position in the head. Nothing had changed on the board, the problem was not yet solved, and yet, in an intuitive flash, complete certainty was attained. "She's got it; I think she's got it," as Professor Higgins would have said.

This curious faculty, so satisfying in puzzles and in mathematics, seems also to be present in faith. It may vary with different people, slow and gentle in some, violent in others, personal to each and, hence, impossible to explain. You may recall the example of C. S. Lewis, who left home in a sidecar not a Christian, and alighted as a Christian at Whipsnade Zoo. Newman, at Littlemore, had just completed, as a parson, the Preface to his *Development of Doctrine;* he had to add a postscript "Since the above was written, the author has joined the Catholic Church." Countless examples might be cited out of which, for special reasons, I have chosen three or four. In a curious way, these picked examples seem to fit the pattern of my book. The men themselves were not priests or bishops but distinguished statesmen and they had this in common, too, that they expressed their views in secret, entirely to assist themselves.

Two of the three kept what our Victorian ancestors would

have known as a commonplace book. In such a book, each jotted down quotations, thoughts, or resolutions that at the time seemed helpful to himself. Indeed, Marcus Aurelius, the Roman Emperor, dedicated his commonplace book "To Himself." It later became famous as *The Meditations,* but the Emperor never intended this. Marcus Aurelius may never have heard of Christ. Marcus Aurelius makes one reference to Christians, but this is generally thought to be an addition and spurious. A devout pagan, a Stoic, searching earnestly for a meaning, he took Plato, Cicero, and Epictetus as his guides. There is a certain sadness about his thoughts, as might be expected in one who knew nothing of Christian hope. Yet, under various titles, the gods, Nature, Providence, conscience, he came remarkably near to the truth. Thus he wrote of conscience, "Remember, it is the secret force hidden deep within us that manipulates our strings; there lies the voice of persuasion, there the very life; there, we might even say is the man himself. Never confuse it in your imagination with its surrounding case of flesh, or the organs adhering thereto, which, save that they grow upon the body, are as much mere instruments as the carpenter's ax. Without the agency that prompts or restrains their motions, the parts themselves are of no more service than her shuttle to the weaver, his pen to the writer, or his whip to the wagoner."[2]

Marcus Aurelius compiled his commonplace book on the Danube while commanding the legions, hard pressed by the barbarians. One biographer describes the scene: "There, among the misty swamps and reedy islands of that melancholy region, he consoled the hours of loneliness by penning the volume of his *Meditations.* Labourious years of toil and conflict had, by now, exhausted his spirit; he was weary of life and, in his own words, 'was waiting for the retreat to sound.'" In fact, he died in that camp soon afterward, on March 17, 180; he had been Emperor for nineteen years and was fifty-nine. His death was edifying, for he wanted no attention in his fever, but was much concerned for his men.

Marcus Aurelius had certainly found a full meaning to life. The last lines in his book have a charm about them not rivaled by the saints. He saw himself as an actor on the stage and God as the producer. "In your drama of life, three acts are all the play. Its point of completeness is determined by him who, formerly, sanctioned your creation and, today, sanctions your dissolution. Neither of these decisions lay within yourself. Pass on your way, then, with a smiling face, under the smile of him who bids you go."

How different were the experiences, nearly two thousand years later, of the Swedish statesman Dag Hammarskjöld. His commonplace book was discovered after Dag had been killed in an air crash; they found it in a drawer of the desk in his New York home.

One friend alone seems to have known of its existence, and Dag himself left on record "It was begun without a thought of anybody else reading it." When *Markings* was published in 1963, it enjoyed sensational sales. This, in itself, tells us of the secret search for meaning; I heard, on a radio talk, that half a million readers, in the first year, bought this very religious book. Hammarskjöld himself was a Lutheran by tradition, but some biographers leave the impression that he was vaguely agnostic in his younger college years. He said much the same himself. He was an economist by training, a successful banker, who went into politics. Outwardly, Dag was highly successful and, as Secretary General of United Nations, he became an international figure, much admired, much overworked, and respected for a dedicated public life. Behind the scenes, we now know that he was lonely and diffident, much tempted at one time to suicide. He never married and, though socially most acceptable, found some difficulty in making intimate friends.

Something happened to Dag. It would perhaps be more accurate to say not that something happened but that someone came to Dag. In 1952 he could write in his private book "What I ask is absurd; that life shall have a meaning. What I strive for, is impossible; that my life should acquire a mean-

111

ing." Yet nine years later, on Whitsunday 1961, he entered in his book, "Once I answered 'Yes' to Someone-or-Something. And from that hour, I was certain that existence is meaningful and that, therefore, my life, in self-surrender, has a goal."

Dag never looked back. He who once wrote in his book,

Too tired for company,
You seek a solitude,
You are too tired to fill,

made almost his last entry on August 2, 1961,

Almighty . . .
Forgive
My doubt

My anger

My pride.

By thy mercy

Abase me,

By thy strictness

Raise me up.

A critic once wrote of *Markings*, "One feels one has read it all before, somewhere, in Meister Eckhart, St. John of the Cross, *The Cloud of Unknowing*, or Juliana of Norwich," but, for all that, it remains remarkable that a professional statesman, immersed in business, should also have found peace by saying "Yes" to Someone and thus enjoying a truly contemplative life.[3]

For our last example of the puzzle coming out, of a problem solved, of the search for meaning, we go back to Tudor

London and to the man for all seasons, Sir Thomas More. Historically, how interesting the problem of gauging and comparing the merits and talents of three remarkable and dedicated men. All three wrote best sellers; Thomas More published *Utopia* in his lifetime; *Markings* and *The Meditations* appeared after the authors' deaths. How compare a Roman Emperor, a Secretary General of United Nations, and a Lord Chancellor of England, a Renaissance scholar, now of worldwide fame? They had in common the search for meaning, the discovery of a fuller meaning that is faith. The Roman Emperor died on the Danube, smiling; the Secretary General perished in a plane crash, happy; he had said "Yes" to Someone in 1961. The Lord Chancellor laid down his life for his faith.

Thomas More was still called Young More when he was fifty; his old father, a high court judge, lived long enough to marry four times. Young More was sensitive, alert, and enthusiastic in boyhood; he was attractive and blushed easily. Later in life, he would write a charming poem to Eliza, "whom he had loved in his youth." Young More had contemplative yearnings in boyhood, and verses survive in which a boy talks to his girl in the first stanza and young More says the same to God in the next. Young More not only thought of the priesthood and of celibacy but, for three years, as a law student, lodged in a Carthusian monastery. He took no vows and chose, in the end, to marry and, in fact, married twice. Everything prospered for him. He became a distinguished lawyer and civic worthy, member of Parliament, Speaker of the House of Commons and, eventually, in sad circumstances, Lord Chancellor. Meanwhile, he had enjoyed a happy home, with his son, his three daughters, his stepdaughter, an adopted daughter; jester, secretaries, tutors, sons-in-law, boatmen, and the rest. His family at Chelsea numbered seventy, and he had a tally of twenty-three grandchildren at the end. Yet, every morning, he rose impossibly early to attend Mass and to say his prayers.

Thomas More, at the peak of his fame, appeared urbane and witty, highly successful in his profession, a famous scholar, and the King's dear friend. He had first met Henry VIII when the future despot was only ten. Later More had access to the royal apartments when Catherine of Aragon was doing the domestic sewing and Henry, in his shirt sleeves, sat back and invited Thomas More to tell him about the stars.

For all his urbanity and wit, Thomas More, the man for all seasons, was a tense and apprehensive man. One of the greatest portrait painters of all times, Hans Holbein, Jr., stayed in Chelsea at Thomas More's house. When Holbein painted the More sketches and portraits, Thomas More was forty-nine. I have the second Holbein sketch over my mantelpiece and inspect it daily; I have to agree, with Professor Brewer, "that the face of More is remarkable for its peering, anxious look, as of a man endeavouring to penetrate into, yet dreading the future"; such an expert verdict reveals the historical facts.[4] Thomas More, for all his piety, wit, and basic goodness, was always a hesitant man. Once he had committed himself, challenged the King, parted in tears from his family to be lodged in the Tower of London, he found the fuller meaning to life and a majestic faith. He himself pinpointed the very moment, as William Roper, his son-in-law, ferried him home to Chelsea from the Privy Council session at Lambeth, at which he had committed himself. More said, "I thank God, son Roper, that the field is won."

Thomas More remained in the Tower of London for fifteen months. He had prematurely aged and had suffered much physical discomfort, but he was the happiest prisoner that the warders had known. Alone in his cell, he wrote his last book, the *Dialogue of Comfort in Tribulation,* with a Hungarian uncle consoling his nephew, afraid of the advance of the Turks. This was pure camouflage. More was consoling his family, and Henry VIII was the Turk. Professor R. W. Chambers picks out the significant point: "More's writings in the Tower of London are more carefree than those which he wrote in freedom; a collection of More's merry tales would draw heavily from the *Dialogue of Comfort*. There is a marked contrast between the happiness of the *Dialogue* and the grim tone of *The Four Last Things,* written when More was rising to power in the King's service."[5]

In the Tower, More suddenly saw the answer to life's puzzle, and he reverted to the theme of his boyhood verses between a boy and his girl. Not so long before his execution on Tower Hill, More wrote feelingly of the joys of heaven and of his willingness to die. He ended, "Then shall I be satiated, satisfied and fulfilled when thy glory, Good Lord, shall appear, with the fruition of the sight of God's glorious majesty, face to face."

The Nicene Creed ends "We look for the resurrection of the dead and the life of the world to come." Newman should have the last word, and one could quote from his *Dream of Gerontius,* tracing the journey of an old man through death to the presence of God. But Newman also penned his own epitaph and this, maybe, sums up a lifetime and expressed his feelings at almost ninety, when he died. He wrote in Latin, which has been translated,

"From the Shadows to Reality."

CHAPTER NOTES

A book as slight as this barely deserves a bibliography, index, references, or notes. Most readers will take all quotations for granted, presuming in the author a love for truth. Past experience, however, underlines the rights of those readers who wish to pursue the subject further or who seek encouragement in the choice of books. Such a praiseworthy aim is heightened here, for AND WOULD YOU BELIEVE IT! relies with some pride on the tracts, books, and sermons of Cardinal Newman, and the hunt for these, as the author knows, proves an exhausting exercise.

One further half-size hurdle has to be cleared. The great Cardinal's writings have appeared in many editions and some of his more famous books are now available in paperback. Where possible and unless otherwise stated, all references are taken from the *Christian Classics Edition,* published from 1966 onwards, Westminster, Maryland.

Chapter One

1. This book is dedicated to the dear friend whose letter is here quoted and who pondered about the Nicene Creed at Sunday Mass.
2. Newman. *Grammar of Assent* p. 132. See also *Parochial and Plain Sermons,* Vol. 2, p. 29, The Incarnation, for the value of the creed as a prayer on Christmas Day.
3. Many books have been written about the origin and history of the various creeds. Newman, in his *Essays and Sketches,* deals with certain scriptural difficulties raised against the creeds. (Longman Green edition, 1948). Vol. 1, p. 201 *seq.* A succinct and scholarly account of the creeds may be found in *A Catholic Dictionary of Theology.* (Thomas Nelson, Inc., Nashville, 1961.) Cf. articles *Arianism* and *Creeds.*
4. Ronald Knox. *The Creed in Slow Motion* (Sheed and Ward, New York, 1949), p. 3.

Chapter Two

1. Newman. *Grammar of Assent.* The Creed is discussed pp. 146–47; the operation of the intellect pp. 101–21.

2. Knox, op. cit., pp. 3–4.
3. Those interested in Cardinal Newman's consistency of thought and teaching throughout a long and varied lifetime should consult William Lamm, O.M. *Newman's Spiritual Legacy* (Bruce Publishing Co., Milwaukee, 1934).
4. Newman, *Grammar of Assent*, p. 390.
5. Ibid., pp. 98–99.
6. Ibid., p. 117. The subject of conscience is further examined pp. 106–21.
7. Charles Stephen Dessain. *The Mind of Cardinal Newman.* (Catholic Truth Society, London, 1974). This admirable little booklet by an expert supplies a succinct and masterful review of Newman's thought. Further, it provides excerpts from Newman's writings, now not easily available.
8. Newman. *Sermons preached on various occasions*, pp. 64–65. The same sermon, delivered some years before at St. Mary's, Oxford, is found in *Parochial and Plain Sermons*, Vol. 2, p. 13 *seq.*
9. Newman. Letter to Mr. Leigh, November 24, 1873. Printed in *A Newman Reader*, F. X. Connolly, p. 312. (Doubleday, Image Books, Garden City, N.Y., 1964).
10. Solzhenitsyn. *The Gulag Archipelago* (Harper & Row, New York, 1974). The quotation given in the text was copied from a newspaper serialization, not easily traced in so long and complicated a book. The great Russian author happily repeats the theme of the birth of conscience frequently as when he writes, "Prison had already undermined my certainty, and the principal thing was that some kind of clean, pure feeling does live within us, existing apart from all our conviction." P. 612.
11. Newman. *Grammar of Assent*, p. 106.
12. Newman. *Occasional Sermons*, p. 74.

Chapter Three

1. Newman, *Grammar of Assent*, p. 192.
2. Ibid., p. 392.
3. Ibid., pp. 390–91, 394.
4. Newman, *Occasional Sermons*, op. cit., p. 66.
5. Newman, *Grammar of Assent*, p. 57.
6. Newman, *Occasional Sermons*, p. 61.
7. Ibid., p. 69.
8. Newman, as clergyman and as tutor at Oxford, devoted many years to the study of the Fathers of the early Church. His sketches of St. Athanasius, St. Basil, and others appeared, first, as articles in learned journals and were later published in book form. Few later writers have written more vividly on the Church of the four first centuries, especially on the Arian heresy. The bulk of his historical research may be found in *Historical Sketches*, Westminster Edition, Vol. 2.

9. Newman. *Apologia pro Vita Sua* (Doubleday, Image Books, Garden City, N.Y., 1956). P. 241.
10. St. Leo's letter to Flavius is often quoted, e.g., *A Catholic Dictionary of Theology;* article *Creeds.* John Hardon, S.J., in his *The Catholic Catechism* (Doubleday, Garden City, N.Y., 1975), pp. 138–40, well describes the situation and modern variants of the controversy.
11. Newman describes the effect of St. Leo's ruling on his personal position in his *Apologia,* op. cit., p. 221.
12. Ibid., p. 217.
13. Kathryn Ann Lindskoog. *Mere Christian* (G/L Publications, Glendale, Calif.), pp. 6–7.

Chapter Four

1. Newman, *Grammar of Assent,* p. 404.
2. Newman, *Parochial and Plain Sermons,* Vol. 3, p. 166.
3. Newman, *Essays Critical and Historical;* quoted here from Dessain, *The Mind of Cardinal Newman,* p. 68.
4. Newman, *Grammar of Assent,* p. 448.

Chapter Five

1. Knox, *The Creed in Slow Motion,* p. 146.
2. Newman, *Select treatises of St. Athanasius;* quoted from Dessain, op. cit., p. 59.
3. Newman, *Grammar of Assent,* p. 132.
4. Knox, op. cit., pp. 145–49.
5. Jerusalem Bible, Introduction, *The Prophets.*
6. Newman, *Parochial and Plain Sermons,* Vol. 2, p. 220.
7. Newman, *Sermons on Subjects of the Day,* p. 23.

Chapter Six

1. Knox, *Enthusiasm* (Clarendon Press, Oxford, 1950), p. 9.
2. Newman, *Discourses to Mixed Congregations,* p. 247.

Epilogue

1. Frankl, Viktor, *Man's Search for Meaning; The Doctor and the Soul; The Unconscious God.* The first two of these books are easily obtained in paperback; the third, published by Simon and Schuster (New York, 1975), throws much light on Consciousness and Conscience from a psychotherapist's point of view. Dr. Frankl's experiences as an eminent psychotherapist and as a prisoner in Auschwitz seem to support and supplement Cardinal Newman's approach to reality.

2. *The Meditations of Marcus Aurelius,* Book X, Section 38. There have been many editions of this Roman classic, written, in fact, in Greek. A. S. A. Farquharson's translation with notes and comments (Clarendon Press, Oxford, 1968) is perhaps the most complete. Penguin Classics provides the rendering of the passage quoted here and many of the details about the Emperor.

3. Dag Hammarskjöld, *Markings* (Alfred A. Knopf, New York, 1964, 13th Impression) has been used in this book. W. H. Auden, the poet, helped with the translation and added biographical notes. One note is critical of Dag, who, in a letter to a friend, saw *Markings* as a true profile of himself. Does such a statement render *Markings* artificial and a pose? While deploring the use of this unhappy expression, the reader may well feel that the integrity of the composer is unhurt.

4. John Sherrin Brewer, *The Reign of Henry VIII* (1884), Vol. 1, p. 292, note. Professor Brewer, in his day the leading expert on Tudor State Papers, formed this opinion of the celebrated portrait of More, by Hans Holbein. Each reader may test the verdict for himself.

5. In recent decades, studies and biographies of Thomas More, the Man for All Seasons, have added greatly to our knowledge of the many phases of his life. Yet few, if any, have surpassed the standard biography by Professor Chambers (Penguin Classics, 1963). The scene in the boat, returning from Lambeth Palace, is given by William Roper, More's son-in-law, who was in the boat with him and lived for some years in More's house. Cf. *Lives of Thomas More.* Roper and Harpsfield p. 80 (Dent, London, Everyman's Edition. No. 19. 1963). *The Dialogue of Comfort* and *Utopia* may be found in Everyman's, No. 461, 1962.

R29